GATHER & GRILL

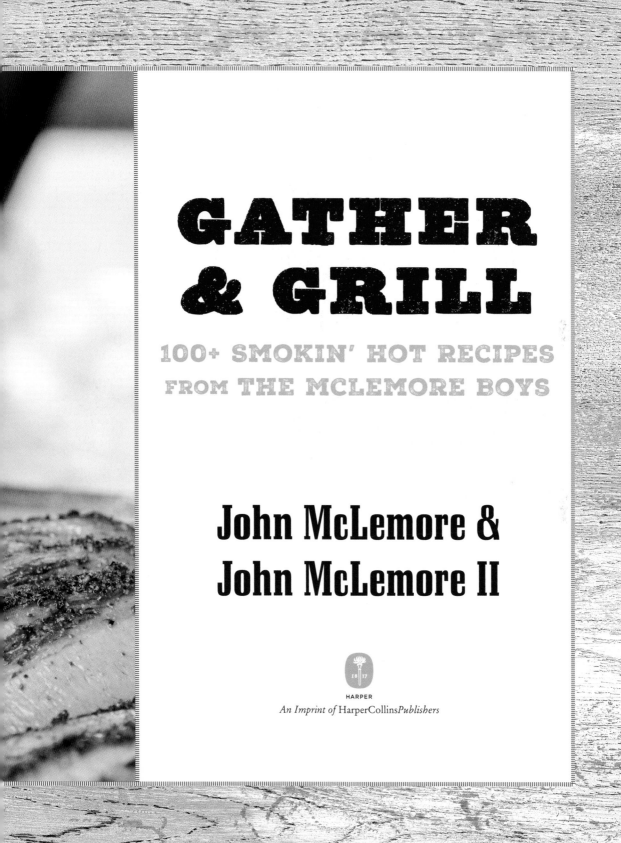

GATHER & GRILL

100+ SMOKIN' HOT RECIPES FROM THE MCLEMORE BOYS

John McLemore &
John McLemore II

HARPER

An Imprint of HarperCollinsPublishers

This book is dedicated to Tonya McLemore, the matriarch of the McLemore family. Tonya Machelle Norman met John Darin McLemore in July 1986, on a blind date set up by their parents. They said "I do" on August 27, 1988, and she started her life as a McLemore, bringing her infectious smile and laughter, sweet personality, and ability to hold us all accountable as a family. She is amazing. She has been instrumental in our success since the day she stepped into our lives. Tonya has NEVER wavered in her love and commitment to her marriage, her family, and her support of a growing family business. The true partnership she offers through every recipe, story, tip, secret, photo session, live cooking event setup and teardown, and family and business decision is priceless. No matter what the task is, Tonya is all in and game to just get it done. We've all heard that everything rises and falls on leadership. We believe that servant leadership separates good leaders from great leaders. That is Tonya McLemore (aka Mom, Mama Mac, and T-Maw).

Thanks, and much love from The McLemore Boys (aka Dad and Johnboy).

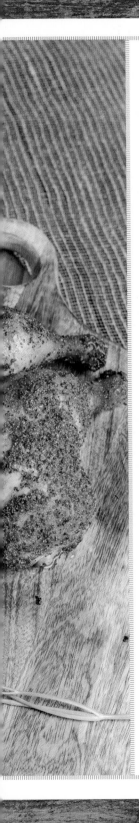

CONTENTS

FOREWORD

If you love great food that's fun to make, you've picked up the right cookbook.

My dad, Jim Doocy, had a lot of fun grilling out on the Kansas prairie. I can still see him standing in our backyard, somewhere inside a crazy cloud of charcoal smoke, tending to T-bones that despite spectacular fat flare-ups were always superbly medium-rare and charred in strategic spots. My dad would say, "It's not burnt, Stephen—that's flavor."

Sixty years later, every time I fire up our backyard BBQ on steak night, I try to replicate that exact flavor—and when I do . . . it tastes like home.

This book is all about the fun of finding that flavor—because backyard grilling and smoking and frying have come a long way since the days my dad would use half a can of lighter fluid on the briquets, shooting up five-foot flames and terrifying our dog, Rags.

A few years ago, when my wife, Kathy, and I started writing our Happy Cookbook series, we called on the McLemores to help us come up with innovative recipes that would pop off the page and prompt people to want to make them. Their ideas worked out better than we could have ever imagined. The week of Thanksgiving in 2020, the most popular turkey recipe in the USA was our first joint project, the Bacon Braided Smoked Turkey Breast. In 2022, the most-searched, most-made, most-loved meatloaf IN THE WORLD was our Grandma's Braided Bacon Meatloaf 2.0.

America fell in love with both of those recipes because the meatloaf and the turkey were both cleverly wrapped in a magnificent BACON weave. The McLemore Boys shared with us the technique of wrapping pork sausage stuffed with assorted deliciousness and covered with a bacon weave, called a Fatty. The combination of pork sausage wrapped with a bacon weave can make you go hog wild! Can this family please be awarded the Nobel Prize for Pork?

You may already know that the McLemores, John and John II, join us every Friday in the summer on *FOX & Friends*, presenting a mouthwatering menu of off-the-charts genius recipes. What you don't know is that long before we start the TV show on those mornings, when I walk into our NY skyscraper at 4 a.m., the McLemores have already fired up their grills and Midtown Manhattan is shrouded in a dreamy haze of barbecue smoke. I'm sure that succulent smell wafts over and drives our neighbors at the *Today* show crazy—it drives me crazy when I'm inside our studio waiting for the McLemores to hurry up and bring us our BBQ brunch at 7 a.m.

This McLemore family has grilling in their genes, and probably knows more about outdoor cooking than just about any other family in America. Back in the 1970s, the family patriarch, Dawson McLemore, was a struggling salesman/inventor. He started building fish fryers in their backyard and sold them out of the back of his truck. A deeply religious fellow, one day Dawson made a deal with the Almighty: "God up there in Heaven, if you could help me sell a bunch of these things so I can feed my family . . . I'll name the company after You."

Guess what . . . the fish fryers started selling like deep-fried hotcakes, so Dawson McLemore knew he had to keep his word and name the company after the Lord. Since God is the Master and Dawson was the company builder, he made the name simple: Master + builder = Masterbuilt. And that's how the world-famous Masterbuilt company was born. To this day, the McLemores' priorities are faith first, family second, and then everything else.

In those early days of the Masterbuilt company, people bought their outdoor cooking machines, but they didn't actually know what to do with them, other than singe steaks like my dad. So the McLemores did a great public service by writing classic American recipes to teach people what you could cook with one of their fryers, smokers, or grills.

Which brings us to today. The McLemores' mission with this cookbook is to share with the world their family's many tricks of the trade and saucy secrets. Take a good look at the ideas in this book, find something that you think looks amazing, and make it! And when it turns out better than you expect— palm it off as your own idea. Trust me, I know the McLemores, and they would love it if one of their recipes wound up in your household's regular rotation. A gift from their family to yours.

So as my kids say . . . let's go! Turn the page, find a recipe, start a fire, and find that flavor!

—Steve Doocy, *FOX & Friends* cohost and coauthor (with his wife, Kathy) of the Happy Cookbook series

From John McLemore

I have had the privilege of working
in a family business my entire life.
I started working with my dad,
Dawson McLemore (whom I call
"Ole Man"), in our backyard when
he was running M & M Welding,
and later worked on building the Masterbuilt brand globally
for nearly fifty years. Now in a whole new capacity that isn't
limited to the walls of Masterbuilt, I'm honored to work with
my son John II. With passion and excitement for cooking,
entertaining, and sharing the goodness we want to show
you what we love to do. I am so proud to share our recipes
and personal stories with all of you as, father and son, we
continue the journey started
by the Ole Man, the original
McLemore Boy.

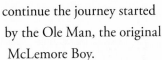

From John McLemore II

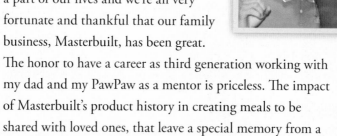

I've also had the privilege of working
with my dad in our family business
since I was fifteen. It's always been
a part of our lives and we're all very
fortunate and thankful that our family
business, Masterbuilt, has been great.
The honor to have a career as third generation working with
my dad and my PawPaw as a mentor is priceless. The impact
of Masterbuilt's product history in creating meals to be
shared with loved ones, that leave a special memory from a
football tailgate, holiday gathering, family reunion, or other
get-together with friends
and family, is inspiring.
I'm excitied to continue
working with my dad and
sharing our journey with
all of you as we keep doing
what we love the most:
cooking, entertaining, and
just having fun.

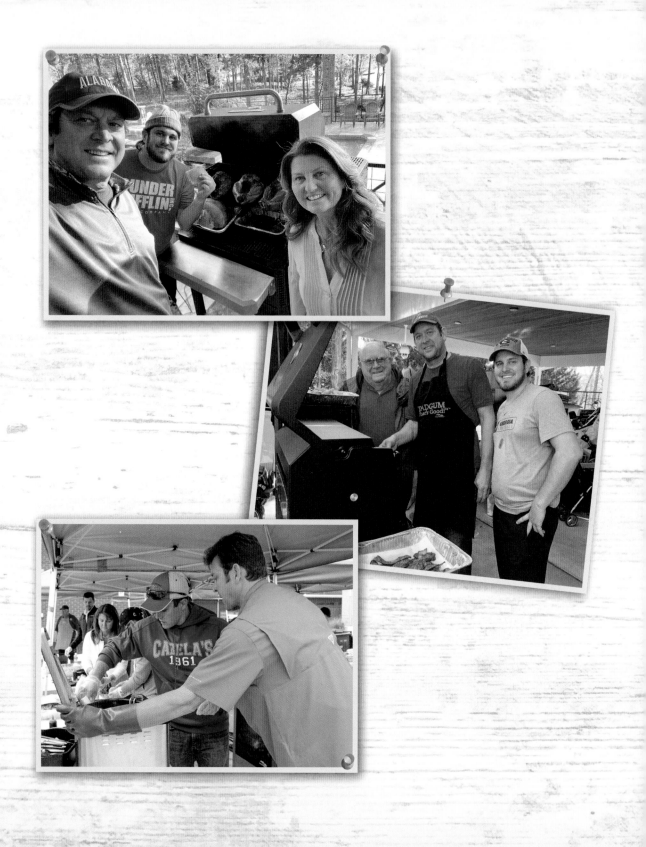

True Backyard Business with The McLemore Boys

When it's time to gather and grill with your family, we hope these recipes and tips will help inspire you to create lasting memories and enjoy great food like we have. From the OG McLemore Boy, the Ole Man/Pawpaw, sharing his thoughts on a paper napkin to us sharing our stories from our family adventures in this cookbook, we hope our passion for cooking is contagious. Our family business and backyard culinary journey are the American dream we've been blessed with. We continually strive to master and share in this social media age a lifetime of knowledge that we hope you'll enjoy. We truly feel these traditional family recipes and creative new ones should be shared for all to enjoy. It started in our backyard over fifty years ago, and we're still in the backyard today. So this book is from our backyard to yours.

Thank you all for allowing us to gather together at your grill.

—The McLemore Boys

INTRODUCTION

Masterbuilt University

It all began with a dream back in 1973. Dawson McLemore was a family man with a wife and five kids. He was a US Navy veteran and worked for Goodyear Tire. His dream was to be his own boss as an entrepreneur. He took a scary leap of faith to start his own business in his backyard, bending and welding steel to build his first product.

That product was a fern stand for his wife, Evelyn, to hold and water their plants at home. Evelyn was the matriarch of the family, MeMaw to all the grandkids, and Dawson's biggest supporter, helping him fulfill his dreams while raising five kids as their new journey began. After a full day's work at Goodyear, Dawson would work to build these fern stands, and people came to love them.

With the teamwork and collaboration of a workforce of seven, it grew enough for Dawson to quit his day job at Goodyear in 1976. A simple fern stand ignited a desire to sell more products that others could use in their own homes just like they did. Fish cookers, bakers' racks, turkey fryers, trailers, hitch hauls, smokers, electric turkey fryers, and grills are a pretty amazing product legacy. Hard work and passion went from being a backyard hobby to a full-time career that supported his entire family. In 1978 Dawson, or "Ole Man," as his kids call him, renamed the company "Masterbuilt" to thank the good Lord (Master) for blessing him with the ability to "build" products to provide for his family.

From the very first day, the whole family got involved, working in the backyard to

build products that were sold locally at first but would later be sold globally. For over fifty years, they enjoyed working in the family business, known for being one of the most innovative companies in the outdoor cooking industry. Creating products that had never existed before is what would separate them from all the rest. They developed a reputation as being pioneers and took great pride in being unique and different. R and D to the McLemores meant

"research and develop," never "research and duplicate." God blessed them with every opportunity they explored, and risk they took. Even when times were uncertain and scary, they always pushed forward and knew it was worth the risk. In the early days each family member had their own specific skill set to get the job done. There was hands-on learning, and the goal was to divide and conquer in order to have the products out on time. Dawson was the president and

designer. Evelyn was the accountant and office manager. Bubba was in sales, Bill was

the shop foreman, Don was distribution and logistics, Donna was an assistant in the office, and John was sales and management. No college degrees among them except for the priceless education of hands-on learning at the University of Masterbuilt!

The team had direct and constant contact with their customers to listen and understand their needs. They were able to spot opportunities for product improvements, manufacture prototypes in a timely manner, and have innovative and creative designs. Their quest for different and better helped them stay ahead of their competition. The boys created products

they loved to use themselves, and still use today. Looking back in time to 1973, John started with his dad in the backyard watching his dad build these fern stands one by one and stacking them up, waiting for the Ole Man to sell them on his weekends

off from Goodyear. Instead of waiting, John decided to venture out on his own at age eight, loading a few fern stands on his little red wagon and selling them door to door around the neighborhood. As time went on, John realized that this backyard hobby of his dad's was something he loved to do as well. John poured his heart and soul into the business as much as he could every day after school and on weekends, electing to work instead of playing sports and doing other activities. John went from loading his wagon at age eight to graduating from high school and loading his truck with products to sell to retail stores in the surrounding states.

This became an obsession with John, not because he was thinking at that time of making money, but because he loved the challenge and the reward the challenge brought him. John has always said that the perfect job is the job you love to do so much,

you would be willing to do it for free, but you do it so well that they pay you.

Fast-forward to 1984: The Ole Man decided to semiretire and turn the reins over to the boys. At age eighteen, John became a part owner in the business and hit the road full-time Monday to Friday selling in the southeastern states. John was a workaholic and obsessed with his career, but he wanted more and needed a partner who understood the dynamics of a family business. He discussed this with his mom and explained that he wanted to meet a good Christian girl who he could share his life with and who wouldn't mind being on a "roller-coaster ride." At twenty-one John met Tonya, the girl of his dreams, on a blind

date set up by their parents. At twenty-two he became the president and CEO of the company and worked to expand the family business outside the southeastern states. A year later, at twenty-three, he got married to Tonya Machelle Norman and started a family. John and Tonya had three kids, Brooke, John II, and Bailey, while growing a family business. They have both said many times that managing a family business and growing a family was challenging at times,

but always worth it. John admitted that his priorities would sometimes get out of order, but Tonya was always there to reel him back in to what was most important: faith and family. John has often said that a successful leader is one who can accomplish all their goals in business and not lose what's most important to them in the process.

As the journey continued, the McLemores found themselves facing different challenges that tested their faith. Whether the challenges were financial, surviving two devastating fires at the manufacturing facility in 1992, or relationships both internal and external, they always relied on their faith in God to get them through it. The McLemores have always been a family and company of faith, and would regularly say that God was the CEO of the company. God has always had His hands on the company, and on the McLemore family. Through all the ups and downs, their faith allowed them to get through any challenge. They prayed before

meetings and events, held Bible studies at the office, even tithed off the profit of the company every year, and God never let them down. They continue today with a Bible study/prayer partner private group on Facebook called The Charcoal Connection.

As the business grew and changed so did the family dynamics inside the walls of Masterbuilt. Things were going to plan, and the company was doing well when the Ole Man decided it was time to fully retire in 1998 and move on to less stressful things in life like huntin' and fishin'. Memaw also

retired, and through the years Bubba, Bill, and Donna pursued other ventures as well. John was CEO and his brother Don was COO, both now fifty-fifty owners. They'd worked together in the company since day one, and for the next fourteen years, both brothers poured everything they had into Masterbuilt. Their partnership took Masterbuilt to a worldwide global brand and has an established reputation as an innovator in the cooking products industry. After much success together, in 2012 Don decided it was time to retire and move on like the Ole Man to hunt, fish, and maybe play a little golf.

This left John at the helm by himself for the first time in forty years. He had always had the support and help of his dad and his brother, but now he was on his own. For the first time since 1973, John was the sole owner. He was ready for the next "degree," but the question was, who would be in this next phase of schooling with him? The answer: his son John II and the incredible team of talented employees that had hung in there with the family. This is where The McLemore Boys' journey really began, and they didn't even know it at the time.

For the next four years, John ran the company, while John II worked with almost every department, from the warehouse to sales, customer service to product development and marketing. John and John II were continuing a company together as father and son. Their goals were to be number one in the products they produced, to be fierce competitors, respected by anyone who worked with them.

They both believe that what goes around comes around, that we all live in a very small world and there's no price you can put on your reputation. This proved to be the right strategy that allowed Masterbuilt to grow and be well respected in the industry.

In 2016, John and his family decided to sell part of the company to a private equity firm called Dominus Capital to help Masterbuilt grow even more. This partnership does just that, helping the company expand its product line and brands with the acquisitions of Smoke Hollow and Kamado Joe.

John stayed on for a few years as CEO of Masterbuilt for Dominus and then the time came for him to step aside and no longer oversee the family business. This was a tough time, and a very different experience for John, but he always knew and trusted that God had a plan, even if he didn't agree or understand it. The time came to sell the balance of the company in December 2021 to a publicly traded company called the Middleby Corporation. This left John and John II without jobs for the first time in their careers. Again, trusting that God had a plan, they looked to Him for guidance on what they needed to do next.

John's "retirement" only started another "degree" at Masterbuilt University. In 2022 he and his son, John II, officially became "The McLemore Boys." They are a dynamic father/son duo who passionately demonstrate their love for gathering and grilling to make it easy and fun for all to do. While John's life's work had been manufacturing and selling cooking products, it's only natural to research and develop using assorted recipes. John's passion to educate and promote his products led to him writing, publishing, and selling three bestselling cookbooks: *DADGUM That's Good* (2010), *DADGUM That's Good, Too* (2012), and *DADGUM That's Good . . . and Healthy!* (2014). Masterbuilt reached the pinnacle of success under the leadership, entrepreneurial guidance, and expertise that John has actually lived and brought to work every day. His faith in God, strong work ethic, and willingness to take risks has blessed him with great success. Over the years, The McLemore Boys have had the privilege to work with some amazing people and companies at different events, like Steve Harvey, Rachael Ray, QVC, *FOX & Friends*, and local TV stations all across the country. They've done radio interviews with Sean Hannity, Bobby Bones, Rick & Bubba, John Boy and Billy, Kix Brooks, Delilah, Mario Lopez, and many others, and podcast

interviews with Sean and Rachel Campos-Duffy, *The BBQ Central Show*, and many other great shows. The table was set for their journey to continue, and these relationships have been a big part of their success—plus, the friendships are what make it fun.

January 2, 2022, John and John II met and discussed next steps for The McLemore Boys. Knowing this day was coming, they had already started exploring different opportunities to start something new. They kept going back to what they loved to do and what they had been doing their entire lives: cooking, entertaining, and having fun. With that in mind, they decided to

become brand ambassadors. Masterbuilt was their first client, and as the founding family of that brand, it was a perfect fit. They started the 2022 season traveling to events at FOX Square for the Super Bowl, at the Daytona 500, and at Talladega, and doing other cooking demos for *FOX & Friends* for holiday events. They both agreed that this was fun and allowed them to do what they truly loved. Traveling to new places, meeting new people, and sharing good food and stories was what The McLemore Boys were all about. The experience of their journey was amazing, and they were looking forward to continuing to work with old and new friends. Things were going well when, with just four and a half months of that new journey under their belts, they got a call from FOX network about cooking for the 2022 *FOX & Friends* All-American Summer Concert Series, which was starting back up after pausing during COVID. The boys remember the call well because it was May 17 and the first concert would be just nine days later on May 26, and FOX needed a quick answer. Without hesitation, the boys said, "We're in, what do we need to do?" Saying yes before they knew how to make it happen is something they've done for most of their careers, but when they make those

quick decisions, you can count on them figuring it out. FOX loved this about The McLemore Boys, which is why they called them in the first place—they're the go-to guys to pull off big events. The boys were

eager and excited to help because it was *FOX & Friends*, who had been great partners with the McLemore family for over twenty-five years. The concert series was fifteen straight weeks, every Friday morning, cooking for 150 VIPs, the FOX hosts, and band members. Masterbuilt, Lane's BBQ, Halteman Family Meats, and other brands joined in to help. The first concert series was a huge success, and FOX wanted more, which was exactly what the boys wanted,

too. They signed up to do it again for 2023 and 2024 and to help the *FOX & Friends* team in any way they could.

The events were going well and the first year was off to a good start for The McLemore Boys and family, and they were not expecting any new surprises. Well, God had another surprise in mind, and his name was Michael Spooner. Michael came into their lives in December 2022, when he wrote a letter to John and explained that he was John's biological son and would like to meet and start a relationship. John had never known about him, and through circumstances that aren't important, Michael

person—a good solid Christian, a family man, and a good cook as well, which was a bonus. This was a good fit for John, Michael, and the family and they were all very thankful for how things were going. After all, God knows what He's doing, right?

This surprise was a great one, and the McLemores are proud to share it any chance they get.

As the events and concert series progressed, and the recipes and stories continued, John and John II thought, *Maybe we should write a cookbook, do it together and tell our story.* Having the recipes and stories in their heads was the easy part—putting it all on paper and capturing it on camera was the harder, more time-consuming part. The boys knew what their strengths and weaknesses

had found out about John in 2015. He waited seven more years before, at forty years old, he finally felt ready to send his letter to John. After reading Michael's letter and processing the reality of this situation, John and Tonya were excited to talk with Michael and meet in person as soon as possible. After meeting in Texas, they both knew that they wanted to build a relationship and focus on the next forty years, not the past. Since connecting in December and meeting shortly after, both John and Michael, as well as their families on both sides, were *all in*. Jana, Michael's wife of nineteen years, and their three kids, Abigail, Alanah, and Ben, along with all the McLemores were ready to build a relationship and never look back. Brooke, John II, and Bailey embraced Michael as the cool big brother they always wanted. Everyone welcomed him into the family with open arms, and it felt so natural. Michael is a worship pastor at Hill Country Bible Church in Austin, Texas, and is truly an amazing

were and how important it was to separate the tasks to deliver this book. They both selected the recipes and spent time testing every single one together. Tonya and the family helped with stories and photos from the past, and the process began. To pull this off, they had to divide and conquer, and they did just that, with John spending more time styling the

food and John II as the tech person behind the camera. Tonya helped with every aspect of the project, but spent most of her time with stories and photos from the past. They had spent a lifetime developing these recipes with family and a few close friends, but had a deadline to meet for the book to go to print, and to meet that deadline, they all had to do their part.

Now teamed up, just like he was with his dad so many years ago, these guys are excited to take you along on their culinary journey. They are incredible communicators with a passion for showing others the ease of cooking simply good recipes that make you want to try it yourself. Their prayer is for you to master assorted recipes, techniques, and products so you can cook some DADGUM good food with your family and friends. The GOODNESS of food, fellowship, time, effort, thankfulness, blessings . . . the list is endless for how being together to share an experience is given and received. A meal without good times with good people is just plain old food. To play a small role in creating memories shared as you gather and grill with your loved ones is priceless. This book is a labor of love, and one The McLemore Boys are very proud of and happy to share with all of you.

Fast-forward from the start of Masterbuilt in 1973 to fifty years later . . .

The McLemore Boys continue to say, "The perfect job is the job you love to do so much, you would be willing to do it for free, but you do it so well that they pay you." They are still living this today, cooking, entertaining, and gathering at the grill with family, friends, and YOU.

TECHNIQUES FOR SMOKING AND GRILLING

Meat and Seafood Selections

Meat

» **Filet Mignon** Cut from the tenderloin, filet is a very tender cut but lacks the beefy flavor of other cuts. Consider grilling this with a good rub or marinade.

» **Flank Steak** A beefy, full-flavored steak cut from the chest and side, this steak is thin and cooks quickly. To retain the juices in the meat, let it rest for a few minutes before carving against the grain.

» **Rib Eye Steak** Cut from the rib, these steaks are very tender, beefy, and well-marbled with fat, which makes them great for grilling and smoking. They should be cut thick and seared over medium-high heat, then moved to a cooler spot on the grill to finish.

» **Sirloin, New York Strip, and Prime Rib** These are full-flavored premium cuts that have a natural flavor, which you may want to bring out with a little salt, pepper, and olive oil.

» **Porterhouse and T-Bone** Cut extra thick, these give you the taste and texture of both the strip and the tenderloin. To prevent it from overcooking, sear the steaks with the strip portion facing the hottest part of the fire and the tenderloins facing the cooler side.

» **Brisket** The brisket consists of two different muscles. The top muscle, known as the point, is fibrous and difficult to cut. The flat is leaner and more even, which makes it easier to cut. It's likely that you'll find the second cut in your local supermarket, trimmed, with a thin layer of fat on the top. If it's untrimmed, trim the fat down to ½-inch thickness. To test your brisket for tenderness, hold the middle of the brisket in your hand. If the ends give on both sides, you've picked a good one. A rigid brisket is a sign that you're in for a tough time.

» **Spareribs** Pick slabs of ribs that weigh between 2 and 4 pounds. Smaller ribs are likely to come from a younger animal and will cook faster because they're more tender.

- » **St. Louis–Style Ribs** These specially trimmed ribs are lighter than spareribs, topping out at about 2 pounds.
- » **Baby Back Ribs** These flavorsome ribs are great if you're smoking for the first time. Baby backs are a little more expensive, but they're the most tender ribs and cook faster than spareribs.
- » **Pork Butts and Picnics** Similar cuts with different bones. There is not much difference between them, but they do offer a choice. You can remove the bone or cook them bone-in.
- » **Sausages** Simple to grill or smoke. If sausage is raw, be sure to cook to proper doneness. For quick and easy smoking or grilling we recommend buying precooked sausage.

> **TIP**
>
> Pork cooked on the bone shrinks less. It also allows you to quickly test for tenderness. When the meat is ready, the bone slides out easily.
>
> Buy your butt with the fat on and trim it to suit your taste. And remember, fat equals flavor.

Seafood

- » **Mahi-Mahi** Similar in texture to swordfish, but a little oilier. Despite this, it dries out quickly on the grill, so you might want to brine it before cooking.
- » **Red Snapper** Quick and easy to grill or fry. If you grill it, handle it carefully. Make sure the fish and the grill are well oiled.
- » **Salmon** A favorite for grilling because it doesn't dry out. It's rich in healthy natural oils and fats, so you can pop it on the grill without oiling. Its flavor also complements stronger marinades.
- » **Scallops** You'll want to use fresh ocean scallops if you're grilling or frying them. Take a close look at the scallops before you buy them. If they're unnaturally white and are sitting in a milky liquid, they're processed. Natural scallops are a pinkish tan or ivory. They have a firmer texture and a bigger surface area that holds batter better if frying.
- » **Trout** Freshwater trout is great on the grill. The skin becomes thin and crispy, and the flesh is flavorsome without an overpowering fishiness.
- » **Tuna** Does best using a simple marinade of herbs and oil. This prevents it from

drying out and getting tough. If you like your tuna rare, buy 1½-inch-thick steaks, which will enable you to sear them without overcooking them.

» **Mussels** Versatile, quick, and cheap. They steam beautifully, and within minutes you can rustle up a satisfying gourmet dish.

» **Shrimp** Tastes great any way you cook it. Though some prefer boiled shrimp, there's a lot to be said for steaming them, which retains their delicate flavor better.

TIP

Fish smokes fast, so it requires a little more attention than beef, pork, or poultry. The best types of fish to test in your smoker are salmon and trout fillets. Boneless fish fillets are the easiest to smoke and eat. Fish with a higher fat content, such as trout, salmon, tuna, and mackerel, retain their moisture better during smoking. Smoke your fish with the skin on, and on aluminum foil to allow it to cook in its on natural juices.

USDA Safe Minimum Internal Temperatures

Beef, Pork, Veal, Lamb (Ground)	160°F
Beef, Pork, Veal, and Lamb (Steaks, Roasts, and Chops)	145°F
Egg Dishes	160°F
Fish	145°F
Turkey, Chicken, and Duck (Whole, Pieces, and Ground)	165°F

Reverse Searing

Reverse searing is a technique that allows you to perfect the internal temperature of your meat while creating that beautifully seared crust on the outside. It essentially means cooking/smoking at a low temperature over indirect heat and then searing at a high temperature over direct heat at the end. You can do this on the smoker and then on a grill or even a griddle for that final sear, or you can also do this at low temperatures in your oven and then sear on the stovetop in a cast-iron skillet. You can smoke all the meat to the same temperature and then use reverse searing for the last few minutes to perfect the desired internal temperature for your crowd and serve all at the same time.

Direct vs. Indirect Grilling

Direct

Direct grilling is a fast method: The heat is high, and the cooking time is shorter. With direct grilling, the food is placed directly above the heat source (whether charcoal, propane, or electric). This grilling method works best for vegetables, hamburgers, or steaks. It's important to stand by your grill and watch the food carefully when using direct heat so it won't burn. Make sure you turn the food as necessary. Close the lid of the grill to get a good sear, but again, don't leave the grill unattended.

Indirect

Indirect heat grilling involves placing your food in a spot on the grill away from the heat source. This means you place the food off to the side, not directly over the coals or flame. You can also place a barrier like a pan or tray between the heat source and the food to redirect the heat, with the added benefit that it can also catch drippings. This is a slower method of grilling, which will require a longer cooking time, but it is much more forgiving. Indirect grilling works great for pork roast, ribs, whole chicken, turkey, and beef brisket.

Most Common Woods for Smoking and Grilling

Whether you're smoking on a small electric smoker on your back porch or in a trailer-size smokehouse, we're sure you can create a DADGUM good result while gathering and grilling! When testing a new wood flavor, make sure you begin with a small amount. If you like the flavor, increase the amount you use when smoking.

Wood Flavors

» **Alder** gives a light flavor that works well with fish and poultry. It's a perfect pairing with salmon.

- » **Apple** gives a very sweet, mild flavor to your food. It pairs well with poultry and pork. Apple wood smoke will turn chicken skin dark brown. It takes a longer cooking time to infuse foods with the flavor of the smoke, so be careful not to oversmoke your food, which will result in a bitter taste.
- » **Cherry** has a mild, sweet flavor and pairs well with most foods. It is great for poultry and fish.
- » **Hickory** will add a strong smoke flavor; be careful not to overuse. This wood pairs best with pork, beef, and lamb. It is available in most areas and is one of the most common woods used for smoking.
- » **Mesquite** is great for smoking and can also be used when grilling. It burns hot and fast, so be prepared to use more wood than you do with other varieties. Mesquite is a great alternative to hickory and has a milder flavor. It pairs well with most meats and is especially good for brisket and hamburgers.
- » **Oak** gives a strong but not overpowering smoke flavor. It pairs well with beef and lamb.
- » **Pecan** burns cooler than other woods and provides a mild flavor. It pairs well with pork and is a great substitute for hickory.

These woods are used for smoking, but are less common: almond, apricot, ash, birch, black walnut, citrus (grapefruit, lemon, orange), crab apple, lilac, maple, mulberry, peach, pear, plum, walnut.

Avoid these woods, as they contain sap and will not give off a complementary taste or smell: cedar, cypress, elm, eucalyptus, fir, pine, redwood, sassafras, spruce, sycamore.

Chips, Chunks, Logs, or Pellets?

The cut of wood you choose depends on the type of equipment you use for smoking. For most large barrel-type smokers or charcoal smokers, you'll want to use chunks. Wood chips are most commonly used for propane and electric smokers. Some grills are equipped with an accessory smoker box for adding wood. Championship BBQ competitors use very large smokers designed to accommodate larger logs or chunks of wood. Pellets are reserved for specialty grills or smokers. There's a difference between the type of pellets used as a heat source versus pellets used for cooking, so make sure you purchase the correct type.

Internal Temperature and Conversion Charts

Beef Internal Doneness Temps

Rare	120°–125°F
Medium-Rare	125°–135°F
Medium	135°–145°F
Medium-Well	145°–160°F
Well-Done	160°–175°F

Pork Internal Doneness Temps

Medium-Rare	Not Advised
Medium	145°–150°F
Medium-Well	150°–155°F
Well-Done	160°–165°F

Chicken Internal Doneness Temps

Done	165°F

Cooking Conversion Chart

MEASURE	FLUID OUNCES	TABLESPOONS	TEASPOONS	LITER (L) MILLILITER (ML)
1 gallon	4 quarts	256 tbsp	768 tsp	3.1 L
4 cups	1 quart	64 tbsp	192 tsp	0.95 L
2 cups	1 pint	32 tbsp	96 tsp	470 mL
1 cup	8 oz	16 tbsp	48 tsp	237 mL
¾ cup	6 oz	12 tbsp	36 tsp	177 mL
⅔ cup	5 oz	11 tbsp	32 tsp	158 mL
½ cup	4 oz	8 tbsp	24 tsp	118 mL
⅓ cup	3 oz	5 tbsp	16 tsp	79 mL
¼ cup	2 oz	4 tbsp	12 tsp	59 mL
⅛ cup	1 oz	2 tbsp	6 tsp	30 mL
1/16 cup	0.5 oz	1 tbsp	3 tsp	15 mL

PART 1

BREAKFAST

At the McLemores', we take breakfast seriously. It's the meal that starts our day—and sometimes gets served at brunch time or even dinner. These recipes are fun and easy to make for a small group any time of the week, for special occasions like camping with friends, or even for a large gathering at the house. Don't just think of traditional bacon and eggs—think bigger.

PRO TIPS

IN THE KITCHEN: Bake the fatty in the oven at 350°F for 60 to 75 minutes, or until the internal temp reaches 160°F. Be sure to place a baking sheet underneath to catch all the drippings.

To add another layer of flavor, drizzle with South Carolina BBQ Sauce (page 83) before cutting.

Breakfast Fatty

SERVES 8

Who doesn't love a good ole breakfast with all the fixins? Start with some savory sausage, ham, cheese, and hearty hash browns, and don't forget the eggs. You can get creative and add whatever breakfast favorites you love from the menu. From bacon to onions, peppers to mushrooms—the possibilities are endless. Making this is part of the fun. Once you have your ingredients assembled, roll it up and smoke away. The aroma will fill the air as you patiently wait for your family to come running to the table. No one can resist a good Breakfast Fatty!

Hickory wood chunks

Extra-virgin olive oil

12 ounces frozen shredded hash browns

4 medium eggs, beaten

Kosher salt and black pepper

2 pounds ground mild pork sausage

1 cup diced cooked ham

½ cup shredded cheddar cheese

Maple syrup

1. Set a grill/smoker to 275°F and add the wood chunks.

2. Lightly coat a medium skillet with olive oil and heat over medium heat. When the pan is hot, add the hash browns and cook according to the package directions. Transfer the hash browns to a large bowl and set aside.

3. Add the eggs to the skillet and scramble until cooked through. Transfer to the bowl with the hash browns and set aside. Feel free to season the hash browns and eggs with salt and pepper to taste. (If you're using a griddle, simply scramble the eggs and brown the hash browns over medium heat, then set aside.)

4. On a sheet of waxed paper, flatten the sausage into a rectangle, roughly 12 x 16 inches.

5. Mix the hash browns and eggs, then place in the center of the sausage and top with the ham and the cheese (feel free to add additional cheese, if desired).

6. Roll the sausage around the eggs, hash browns, ham, and cheese, form it into a log, and pinch both ends to seal. Season with salt and pepper, and drizzle with maple syrup. Leave the roll on the waxed paper to make it easier to transfer to the grill/smoker.

7. Grill/smoke on the middle rack over indirect heat for 1 hour, then place a pan below the fatty log and drizzle again with syrup. Cook for another hour, or until the internal temp reaches 160°F.

8. Slice crosswise into 1-inch-thick pieces and drizzle with more syrup to taste, then serve.

Mini Blueberry Breakfast Fatty

SERVES 8

Our friends from Lane's BBQ in Bethlehem, Georgia, first introduced us to this delicious and creative recipe. We loved it so much, we decided to serve it to the hosts and VIP guests at the *FOX & Friends* All-American Summer Concert Series, and it was a fan favorite! With its sweet and salty combination, it's one of our favorite ways to start the morning or break up an all-day grilling session. It's the perfect marriage of our classic breakfast sausage mix and blueberries, which gives it a burst of flavor. You won't find a breakfast treat quite like this anywhere else. So go ahead and try it—we guarantee your taste buds won't regret it!

2 pounds ground mild pork sausage

8 Hostess Blueberry Muffins or Muffin Sticks

Kosher salt and black pepper

Lane's BBQ apple pie seasoning

Maple syrup

South Carolina BBQ Sauce (page 83; optional)

1. Set a grill/smoker to 275°F.

2. On a sheet of waxed paper, flatten the sausage into 8 rectangles, roughly 4 x 6 inches each.

3. Place 1 muffin stick on each sausage rectangle, season to taste with salt, pepper, and/or apple pie seasoning, and drizzle with maple syrup.

4. Roll the sausage around the muffin stick to form it into a small log, fully enclosing both ends of muffin in the sausage. Feel free to season the outside to taste.

5. Smoke over indirect heat for 30 minutes, then drizzle with syrup. Continue cooking for another 30 minutes (total of 1 hour) or until internal temp reaches 160°F.

6. Slice into 1-inch-thick pieces and drizzle with more syrup or South Carolina BBQ sauce as desired.

PRO TIPS

IN THE KITCHEN: Bake the mini fatties in the oven directly on the middle rack at 350°F for 30 to 45 minutes, until their internal temp reaches 160°F. Be sure to place a baking sheet underneath to catch all the drippings.

Feel free to crumble up a blueberry muffin and use as your blueberry stick that you wrap your fatty around.

PRO TIPS

Top the quesadilla with your favorite hot sauce. Layer on cilantro to taste, inside or outside.

If flipping a whole tortilla is daunting, fill half the tortilla and fold the other half over the filling to form a half-moon. It tastes the same, and it's easier to flip.

★ ★ ★ ★ ★ ★ ★ ★ ★ ★ ★ ★ ★
WAKE FOR WARRIORS

Breakfast Quesadilla

The McLemore Boys were blessed to share this flavorful recipe with participants at a Wake for Warriors event. Founder Dave Deep provides a therapeutic experience for veterans and their families through the transformative power of water sports. Wounded warrior *FOX & Friends* contributor Joey Jones came to our home on Lake Harding, Georgia, to support and participate in this community experience. We decided that the combination of savory and slightly spicy ingredients in this quesadilla are sure to wake you up just like it did for all the veterans and volunteers!

Between the sausage, eggs, cheese, peppers, and onions, there's plenty of flavor. You can even add a dollop of sour cream or guacamole on top as an extra treat! Feel free to customize your quesadilla with other ingredients like spinach, mushrooms, tomatoes, and more. Experiment with different combinations until you find the perfect one for you.

For more information visit wakeforwarriors.org.

Extra-virgin olive oil

1 stick salted butter, plus more as needed

1 green bell pepper, diced

1 red bell pepper, diced

1 small yellow onion, diced

2 jalapeños, seeded and chopped

Kosher salt and black pepper

1 pound ground mild pork sausage

8 large eggs

2 large soft tortilla shells (or burrito-style tortillas, if desired)

Shredded Mexican-style cheese blend

Chopped fresh cilantro (optional)

1. Heat a griddle to medium-high and coat with olive oil.

2. Melt the butter on the griddle and then add the bell peppers, onion, and jalapeños. Season with salt and black pepper to taste. Cook until soft, 6 to 10 minutes, and push to the side of the griddle on low heat or remove.

3. Add the sausage to the griddle and brown until no more pink can be seen, then mix in the vegetables and push the mixture to the side of the griddle to keep warm.

4. Add the eggs to the griddle and scramble. Mix evenly with the sausage and vegetables, then push to the side to keep warm.

5. Melt a little more butter on the griddle to prevent the tortillas from sticking, then place a tortilla on the griddle and top with a layer of cheese. Place the sausage mixture on top of the cheese and add an additional layer of cheese on top. Place the second tortilla on top to make the quesadilla.

6. Cook for 2 to 3 minutes per side, until browned on both sides, flip as needed.

7. Slice like a pizza into sizes that fit your crowd. Garnish with cilantro, if desired.

Smoked BLT

SERVES 4

BLTs are a timeless staple, and at our house, we like them best at breakfast! Plus, because we smoke the bacon, there's no mess of pan-frying on your stovetop. To make this classic sandwich even more special, we take freshly sliced tomatoes and put them on the grill until they're just soft enough to melt in your mouth. Layered with crisp lettuce, thick smoked bacon, and a bit of salt and pepper for that extra zing, this BLT is sure to satisfy everyone's hunger. Happy eating!

1 pound thick-cut bacon, cut in half

2 large tomatoes

8 slices potato bread

Mayonnaise

1 head of lettuce

Kosher salt and black pepper

1. Set a grill/smoker to 350°F.

2. Smoke the bacon over indirect heat for 30 minutes, or until crispy. Remove from the heat and transfer to a plate to cool.

3. Slice the tomatoes to your desired thickness and grill for 2 to 3 minutes on each side, then remove from the heat.

4. While the tomatoes are cooking, toast the bread directly on the grill until browned on both sides.

5. Spread mayo over the bread slices. On half the slices, layer some bacon, lettuce, tomato, salt and pepper, and more bacon on top, and finish with a second slice of bread.

PRO TIPS

Take your smoked BLT to another level by adding your favorite BBQ seasoning to the bacon before putting it on the smoker.

Top with a fried egg to make this sandwich even heartier!

Baked Breakfast Croissant Ring

SERVES 8

The crew from *FOX & Friends* and FOX Weather were in for a real treat on race day at Daytona in 2023 as we whipped up this special recipe. We used our pizza oven to make the ultimate breakfast surprise—a baked breakfast croissant ring! It's an easy and delicious breakfast that packs tons of flavor, and the FOX crew were thrilled with it. Of course, it drew quite a crowd from our camping neighbors as well. We have to admit, it was pretty cool to see everyone enjoying our creation. After all, baking is an art form, and we take pride in making sure that everyone gets the most delicious meals at every race. If you don't have a pizza oven, don't worry—a grill works just as well. Next time you're in Daytona—or at any other racetrack, for that matter—fuel your race day with this delicious recipe. You won't regret it!

Extra-virgin olive oil

1 pound ground mild pork sausage

1 pound thick-cut bacon

8 ounces frozen shredded hash browns

8 large eggs, beaten

2 (8-count) cans refrigerated crescent rolls

Kosher salt and black pepper

2 cups shredded mild cheddar cheese

4 tablespoons (½ stick) butter, melted

1. Set a grill/pizza oven to 400°F. Line a baking sheet with parchment paper.

2. Set griddle heat to medium and lightly coat with olive oil. Use a skillet on the stove as an alternative.

3. Griddle the sausage until you don't see any more pink, push to the side to keep warm. Cook the bacon to your preferred crispiness. Drain the bacon grease and set bacon aside. Finely chop the bacon to create bacon bits.

4. Griddle hash browns to desired crispiness and set to the side.

5. Clean off the griddle or skillet, then add the eggs and scramble until they are no longer runny.

6. Unroll the crescent rolls on a flat surface, separating each triangle, and arrange them in a circle on the prepared baking sheet, with pointy ends facing outward and the bases of the triangles overlapping at the center. The complete ring should form a circle roughly 12 inches in diameter.

7. In even layers, top the base of the triangles with the crumbled sausage, bacon bits, hash browns, scrambled eggs, and salt and pepper all the way around the crescent roll ring. Scatter the cheese over the top and fold the triangle tips over the filling (there will be gaps where ingredients peek out between triangles).

8. Brush the dough with the melted butter.

9. This is where your grill/pizza oven comes into play: Bake for 8 to 10 minutes, be sure to rotate the baking sheet back to front halfway through to ensure no sides get burnt if there are hot spots in your cooking chamber, and bake until golden brown, another 6 to 8 minutes.

PRO TIPS

Elevate the flavor by scrambling your eggs in a little of the grease left over from cooking the sausage and bacon.

You can use premade bacon bits and spray butter to help speed up the recipe.

Smoked Bacon and Egg Cupcake

SERVES 6

When our extended family visits us from Jacksonville, Florida, they always bring good times, and great food ideas. On their last trip, Aunt Helen and cousins Kim, Steve, Robin, Rusty, Ken, and Jeana didn't just share stories—they also shared some fun recipes. This dish was one that Ken and Jeana always cook when they go camping, so we tried it as well while we were camping in Talladega at the spring 2023 race. It was a big winner with all our racing friends. Life doesn't get much better than when you put bacon and eggs on the grill and serve it up!

12 extra-thick-cut bacon strips

12 large eggs

Kosher salt and black pepper

Muffin pan

Cupcake paper liners

1. Set a grill/smoker to 350°F. Line a standard muffin pan with paper liners (no need to grease it).

2. Place the bacon on the middle rack of the grill/smoker. Place an aluminum pan under the bacon to catch the drippings and smoke the bacon until golden brown, about 20 minutes. It's key to not overcook the bacon; you want it to remain "bendy."

3. Remove the bacon from the smoker, blot it with paper towels, and place one piece inside each muffin cup, forming a ring. Crack 1 egg into each bacon ring and season with salt and pepper to taste.

4. Place the muffin pan on the middle rack of the grill/smoker and cook for 20 to 25 minutes, until the egg is done to your liking. Remove from the pan and enjoy.

PRO TIPS

For all you scrambled-egg lovers, you can scramble the eggs before pouring them into each bacon ring, then serve them with cheese on top, a side of grits, and your favorite cup of coffee.

Ultimate Smoked Breakfast Burger

SERVES 4

Put your burger-eating skills to the test with this loaded breakfast burger. Our friend and Fox News host Pete Hegseth was a gamer as he tackled this challenge, at the 2022 Daytona 500 race, like he does every time we come to New York. Stack up the smoked beef patties, double bacon, sausage, tomatoes, and onions, top it off with an egg, and you'll have one big meal! But it's not just about size—it's all about flavor. With every bite, you'll get a unique mix of savory and smoky goodness. It's truly an experience like no other. If you're looking for a delicious adventure, the Ultimate Smoked Breakfast Burger is just what you need! Are you up for a challenge?

2 pounds 80/20 ground beef

2 pounds ground mild pork sausage

Kosher salt and black pepper

Garlic powder

1 pound thick-cut bacon, cut strips in half

2 plum tomatoes, sliced ½ inch thick

4 tablespoons (½ stick) butter

8 slices potato bread or Texas toast

4 large eggs

Mayonnaise

1 large red onion, cut into rings (optional)

1. Heat a griddle to high.

2. Using your hands, form the ground beef into 4 large patties, then do the same with the pork sausage. Season both sides of the patties with salt, pepper, and garlic powder to taste.

3. Griddle the patties for 8 to 10 minutes on each side, or to medium doneness. Pull off the griddle and set on a plate to rest.

4. Add the bacon and tomatoes to the griddle. Cook the tomatoes for 30 seconds per side. Cook the bacon to your desired crispiness, then remove from the heat and place in a small pan to keep warm.

5. Butter the bread lightly to taste and toast it on the griddle, buttered-side down, for 2 to 4 minutes.

6. Melt butter on the griddle. Add the eggs and fry to sunny-side-up doneness. Transfer to a plate.

7. Build each burger, starting with a slice of bread, a smear of mayo, a burger patty, 4 slices of bacon, a sausage patty, more bacon, some tomato, onions (if you like), an egg, and a second slice bread. Enjoy!

> **PRO TIPS**
>
> Try using Come Back Sauce (page 84) instead of mayo for extra tanginess.
>   Top the burger patties with your favorite cheese to add another layer of flavor!

PART 2
APPETIZERS

Appetizers are what kick off a good meal and set the tone for the food that's coming. So when we serve appetizers at the McLemore house, we want everyone happy and ready to see what's next. Hopefully they've never had it and can't wait to try it and then we can hear them say that it's DADGUM good. These apps often steal the show at our events, and it's always fun to hear the buzz that The McLemore Boys have done it again! Whether you're feeding a big crowd or hosting friends and family, these starters are sure to create some buzz, and maybe even steal the show.

PRO TIPS

Buy 1-gallon cans of precooked peanuts at club stores or supercenters to save money. This also shortens the cook time, if you're running short—instead of cooking for 3 to 8 hours, you can simply boil or smoke the peanuts for an hour or so, just long enough to heat up the peanuts and infuse them with flavor.

Boiled, Smoked, and Cajun-Style Peanuts

SERVES A BUNCH

Boiled peanuts are always on the McLemore family's grocery list. Chris, Tonya's late brother, passed on the torch of the peanut king down to John II. Whether it's a camping trip or a family gathering, we always have plenty of peanuts on hand. Recently, we've started spicing up our household staple with Cajun seasoning and some smoke! With bold flavors and unique textures, these creative takes on traditional boiled peanuts are sure to be a hit at any gathering, but they're great for just plain ol' snacking, too. Because this recipe makes a big batch, you'll always have some extra for travel snacks and munching on the way home after a full day of fun!

Boiled or Smoked Peanuts

5 pounds whole raw peanuts, in shell

2 garlic cloves, finely grated

2 lemons, quartered

1 cup orange juice

2 tablespoons distilled white vinegar

4 teaspoons kosher salt

Fresh cilantro leaves, for garnish

Hickory wood chunks, for smoking (optional)

Boiled Peanut Instructions

1. In medium pot, combine the peanuts, garlic, lemon quarters (unsqueezed), orange juice, vinegar, and salt and fill with enough water to cover the peanuts.

2. Stir thoroughly, cover, and simmer over medium heat for a minimum of 2 to 3 hours, or 5 to 8 hours for best results (the longer you cook them, the softer the peanut). Be sure to stir occasionally and add water as needed.

3. Using a slotted spoon, transfer the peanuts to a serving bowl. Ladle the liquid from the pot over the top and garnish with the cilantro.

Smoked Peanut Instructions

1. Set a grill or smoker to 350°F. Be sure to add your favorite wood chunks so the smoke will flavor the peanuts!

2. In a 9 x 13-inch aluminum pan, combine the peanuts, garlic, lemon quarters (unsqueezed), orange juice, vinegar, and salt and add enough water to cover the peanuts. Stir thoroughly to combine.

3. Put the pan directly on the grill/smoker grate and smoke for a minimum of 2 to 3 hours, or 5 to 8 hours for best results (the longer you cook them, the softer the peanut). Be sure to stir occasionally and check the pot every 30 to 45 minutes to see if it needs more water, as some will evaporate.

Cajun Peanuts

1 cup sour orange juice

2 garlic cloves, finely grated

¼ cup hot sauce

2 tablespoons Cajun seasoning

2 tablespoons distilled white vinegar

4 teaspoons kosher salt

5 pounds whole raw peanuts, in shell

2 jalapeños, diced

Fresh cilantro leaves, for garnish

4. Using a slotted spoon, transfer the peanuts to a serving bowl. Ladle some of the liquid from the pan over the top and garnish with the cilantro.

Cajun Peanut Instructions

1. In a large bowl, whisk together the sour orange juice, garlic, hot sauce, Cajun seasoning, vinegar, salt, peanuts, jalapeños, and 6 cups water (or enough to cover peanuts). Cover and refrigerate for at least 8 hours or preferably overnight.

2. Stir thoroughly and transfer to a large pot. Bring the peanut mixture to a boil over medium-high heat, then reduce the heat to maintain a simmer and cook for at least 2 to 3 hours, or 5 to 8 hours for best results (the longer you cook them, the softer the peanut). Be sure to stir occasionally and check the pot every 30 to 45 minutes to see if it needs more water, as some will evaporate.

3. Using a slotted spoon, transfer the peanuts to a serving bowl. Ladle some of the liquid from the pot over the top and garnish with the cilantro.

Johnboy's Slow-Smoked Beef Jerky

Over the past several years, Johnboy has been working on perfecting his slow-smoked beef jerky. This recipe is a time-tested family favorite, passed down to him from Papa Wes, Tonya's daddy. We like to cook it low and slow with our special blend of spices, just like Papa Wes taught us. We lost him in 2010 to lung cancer, and he would surely be so proud of Tonya and all our kids today. Our "secret" spice blend gives this jerky a unique flavor with just the right amount of sweetness and spice that you won't find anywhere else. The smoke from the wood chips creates an unforgettable aroma that always brings back memories of special times with family.

1 (2-pound) beef eye of round roast

2 cups (16 ounces) dark steak marinade (we recommend Dale's Seasoning)

¼ cup Lane's BBQ Q-Nami Rub/Seasoning, or your favorite Asian-style seasoning

Apple wood chunks

2 beers (we recommend standard light beer)

1. Cut the roast into ¼-inch-thick slices and place them in a 1-gallon zip-lock bag. (If you like thicker slices, keep in mind that they'll need additional time on the smoker.) Pour in the marinade, completely covering the meat, and add seasoning to taste. Seal the bag, removing all the air pockets, and massage the bag to ensure the marinade coats all sides of each piece of meat; you want to avoid pieces sticking together and having dry spots on them. Place the bag in a pan in case it leaks and refrigerate for a minimum of 2 hours or up to overnight.

2. Set a grill/smoker to 160°F and add the wood chunks. We recommend going heavier on the smoke to help cure the beef.

PRO TIPS

Set a water pan underneath your jerky for 2 reasons: (1) to ensure the jerky does not have any direct heat hitting it, and (2) adding a beer to the pan helps create an acidic cooking chamber for your jerky, it will help tenderize the meat.

Don't allow jerky to overcook and get too dry and hard, and remember to save a little beer to enjoy with the jerky.

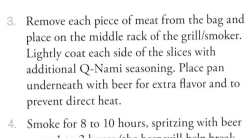

3. Remove each piece of meat from the bag and place on the middle rack of the grill/smoker. Lightly coat each side of the slices with additional Q-Nami seasoning. Place pan underneath with beer for extra flavor and to prevent direct heat.

4. Smoke for 8 to 10 hours, spritzing with beer every 1 to 2 hours (the beer will help break down and tenderize the meat), until the jerky slices are cured but not completely dried out. You want each piece to be slightly bendy.

Smoked Pigs in a Blanket

SERVES 8

When our father-and-son friends Brad and Hudson Terrell joined us at the FOX summer concert series, we decided to get creative with the smoked pigs in a blanket that we were serving to the VIPs. Hudson owns an amazing restaurant in Columbus, Georgia, called the Animal Farm, and this is a favorite appetizer among his customers. We added Hudson's famous homemade whole-grain mustard sauce and served this up as a special treat for the VIPs. It was an instant hit, and everyone wanted to know where they could get these amazing appetizers! We quickly realized that this was something special and worth sharing with the world. It's definitely one of our favorite recipes, and it can easily be made at home, so give it a try and let us know what you think!

1 (8-ounce) can refrigerated croissant rolls

2 pounds Conecuh Sausage, cut into 2-inch pieces

Whole-Grain Mustard Sauce (page 84)

1. Set a grill/smoker to 350°F. Line a baking sheet with parchment paper.

2. Open the croissants into one flat sheet, being sure not to separate them along the perforated lines. Using a knife, cut 1-inch-wide strips of the croissant dough just long enough to wrap around the sausage pieces about one and a half times. Wrap the sausage pieces in the dough strips, placing them on the prepared baking sheet, about 1 inch apart, as you go.

3. Place the baking sheet on the middle rack of the grill/smoker. Cook for 25 to 30 minutes, until the rolls are cooked through and golden brown.

4. Serve with Whole-Grain Mustard Sauce for dipping.

PRO TIPS

Add your favorite spicy BBQ seasoning and/or hot sauce when tossing the hot dogs on the griddle for some extra kick.

Smoked and Griddled Hot Dog Bites

SERVES 8

What we love most about traveling is not what we see, but who we meet. We were set up next to the Travis Pastrana race team at the 2023 Daytona 500 for our *FOX & Friends* segments. The race team was gifted with two hundred beef hot dogs by a sponsor, but no buns and no condiments. They were thrilled to meet us and see if we could help with cooking them. It was a win-win! With some quick thinking, we smoked them for an hour, cut them into bite-size pieces, put them on the griddle with some BBQ rub and sauce, and served them up as an appetizer for a big crowd. This experience taught us that even with simple ingredients like beef hot dogs, you can make something extraordinary. This recipe is now a staple in our cooking repertoire, and we love to whip them up for special occasions! They're always a hit with the crowd, and they're so simple to make.

8 large beef hot dogs

Alabama White Sauce (page 80)

Your favorite hot sauce (optional)

1. Set a grill/smoker to 225°F.

2. Place the hot dogs on the middle rack, making sure they are not touching each other, and place a pan under them to ensure no direct heat is hitting them. Smoke over indirect heat for 1 hour.

3. Remove the hot dogs and cut into 1-inch pieces. Place them on a griddle or in a cast-iron skillet over medium-high heat and cook, tossing them frequently for 8 to 10 minutes.

4. While on the griddle, add Alabama white sauce, and if you want a kick, add your favorite hot sauce, and continue cooking for 2 to 3 minutes.

Griddled Donut BLD

Breakfast. Lunch. Dinner. BLD. You don't have to be a professional chef to make this griddled donut BLD. All it takes is some love, imagination, and the right ingredients—or knowing the right people. Our friend and BBQ expert Ryan Lane of Lane's BBQ is just the right guy. Together we created this fun twist on classic flavors that will leave your taste buds going wild! The combination of our award-winning brisket, homemade pimento cheese, and glazed donuts creates an unforgettable flavor experience. Every time you serve this sweet and savory appetizer, your guests will be begging for more. So don't wait—get griddling!

12 glazed donuts (we recommend Krispy Kreme)

10 slices cooked brisket (see page 111)

10 ounces Spicy Pimento Cheese (page 36), or store-bought

1. Heat a griddle to medium.

2. Take 2 donuts and cut each into 5 pieces (you should have 10 little triangular pieces in total). Place the triangle piece in the hole of the remaining 10 donuts (this prevents your ingredients from falling through the center of your donut sandwich).

3. Griddle 5 slices of brisket for 1 minute to heat them up and then add slices to 5 of the donuts on the griddle.

4. Spread pimento cheese on top of each slice of brisket and top with a second donut. Griddle for 1 minute on each side to melt the glaze and the cheese. Remove from the heat and serve!

Smoked Loaded Glizzy

If you love sausage, bacon, eggs, and French toast, you're going to love this recipe. Everyone has had these ingredients separately, but you haven't lived until you've rolled them all up into one delicious treat—and with the extra smoky flavor, this quickly becomes a masterpiece. This recipe is truly a work of art that the kids will love—and the adults will fight to have their share. The good thing about the Glizzy, it's like festival and fair food, there's always enough to go around, so enjoy—and no fighting! Well, maybe a little bit.

Apple or cherry (sweet) wood chunks

1 pound ground mild pork sausage

1 pound thick-cut hickory-smoked bacon

8 large eggs

¼ cup of your favorite liquid coffee creamer

1 teaspoon vanilla extract

½ teaspoon ground cinnamon

½ teaspoon ground nutmeg

8 hot dog buns

Your favorite shredded cheese

Maple syrup, for serving

Powdered sugar, for dusting

1. Set a grill to 375°F and add the wood chunks.

2. Roll the ground pork into a log the size and length of a standard hot dog, then wrap in bacon (2 slices per log) to help hold the pork together.

3. Place the bacon-wrapped pork dogs on the middle rack of the grill/smoker and place an aluminum pan under them to catch grease. Cook for 30 to 45 minutes, or until the internal temperature reaches 145°F; the sausage should not have any pink left in it.

4. Heat a griddle to medium heat.

5. In a medium bowl, mix together 4 eggs, the creamer, vanilla, cinnamon, and nutmeg to make an egg wash.

6. Dip the hot dog buns in the egg wash and griddle until golden brown (treat it like you're making French toast).

7. Griddle up the remaining eggs, adding cheese if you want.

8. Remove the "French" toasted buns and lay them flat. Top evenly with the eggs and then add a bacon-wrapped pork dog. Drizzle with syrup and dust with powdered sugar. Serve and enjoy!

PRO TIPS
Defibrillator optional.

Mom's Smoked Button Mushroom Bites

Our McLemore matriarch, Tonya, John's wife and John II's mom, was a huge help to us while we were writing and developing this cookbook. This delicious recipe is one of her contributions. One day, we had extra mushrooms in the fridge, and she remembered a recipe she had gotten years ago from a tennis friend. We love learning new recipes from family and friends, and making them our own. This one was quick, easy, and "served" up well. Part of the fun in cooking is experimenting and creating something different. We love mushrooms, cheese, and bacon, so why not put them all together and smoke them? After all, "smoking" certain mushrooms is not always approved by moms, but this one is.

Thanks, Mom.

18 to 20 baby button mushrooms, stemmed

1 (8-ounce) block cream cheese, softened

⅓ cup bacon bits (store-bought)

½ cup sharp cheddar cheese

1. Set a grill to 350°F.

2. Remove stems from mushroom and save for sautéing (see Pro Tip). In a medium bowl, stir together the cream cheese, bacon bits, and cheddar to combine evenly. Generously fill each mushroom cap with the cream cheese mixture.

3. Place directly on the middle rack and grill over indirect heat for 30 to 40 minutes, until the cheese has melted.

PRO TIPS

To avoid lumpy filling, make sure your cream cheese is softened.

Chop up and sauté mushroom stems in butter and garlic, then add them to the cream cheese mixture before stuffing the caps.

Add your favorite seasoning to the cream cheese mixture to give it a little extra pizzazz.

Placing a pan underneath your bites when they're on the grill will help keep the heat indirect and prevent the bottoms from burning.

Baked Personal Pizza Ring

SERVES 8

At the McLemores', pizza is our easy, go-to meal that we pull out of the freezer and heat up for the grandkids when we don't feel like cooking. But when we have the extra time and want to get creative, this is a great option. And if you love fresh-baked crescent rolls as much as we do, you'll love this recipe. This dish is the perfect way to make an at-home meal for the whole family. It's easy to customize with your favorite pizza toppings and cheese, and you can not only get creative with pizza ingredients but also incorporate breakfast, lunch, dinner, and dessert ingredients into the mix. The golden brown buttery crescent roll base of your ring pairs perfectly with the toppings for a delicious meal. Plus, if you have picky eaters in the family, they can customize their own pizza ring, so everyone is happy. So why wait? Try out this recipe tonight and get creative! You won't be disappointed. Happy cooking!

1 pound ground mild Italian sausage

¾ cup thick-cut pepperoni slices (about 6 ounces)

2 cups shredded Colby Jack pizza cheese (about 16 ounces)

2 cups pizza sauce

2 (8-count) cans refrigerated crescent rolls

4 tablespoons (½ stick) butter, melted

¼ cup grated Parmesan cheese

1. Set a grill/pizza oven to 400°F. Line a baking sheet with parchment paper.

2. On a griddle or in a medium skillet over medium heat, cook the sausage until there is no pink left, crumbling it and breaking it up with a wooden spoon as it cooks. Drain the grease from the sausage and place in a medium bowl.

3. Set aside roughly 16 pepperoni for topping and finely chop the rest.

4. In medium bowl, stir together the cooked sausage, chopped pepperoni, cheese, and half the pizza sauce.

5. Unroll the crescent rolls, separating each triangle. Arrange the triangles on the prepared pan in a circle, with the pointy ends facing outward and the bases of the triangles overlapping in the center.

6. Spoon the remaining pizza sauce evenly on each crescent roll triangle as a base layer, try not to spill because it can get messy. Place some of the sausage mixture at the base of each triangle and top with the remaining cheese.

7. Fold the triangle tips over the filling and tuck the tips inside (some filling will peek out between triangles; this is normal).

8. Lightly brush the dough with melted butter, then top with the remaining pepperoni similar to how you'd top a pizza.

9. Bake for 8 to 10 minutes, then rotate the baking sheet back to front to ensure even cooking and bake for 6 to 10 minutes more, until golden brown. Sprinkle top with Parmesan cheese.

PRO TIPS

Instead of melting butter, feel free to use spray butter to spritz the top of pizza ring.

Check out our Baked Breakfast Croissant Ring (page 10).

Spicy Pimento Cheese

SERVES 8

There's nothing better than good ol' Southern-style pimento cheese. With this recipe, we decided to take things up a notch and add some spice to that cheesy goodness with some jalapeños. This legendary pimento cheese pairs perfectly with our pork belly recipe on page 46—or just serve it up with Fritos Scoops for the perfect appetizer when you're entertaining. Trust us, your taste buds will be thanking you for this out-of-this-world combination.

Your favorite wood chunks (we recommend hickory)

2 cups grated sharp cheddar cheese

1 cup grated Colby Jack cheese

½ cup cream cheese, softened

¼ cup Alouette Sundried Tomato & Basil cheese spread (or your favorite variety)

¾ cup mayonnaise

½ cup diced pimentos (do not drain)

¼ cup diced jalapeños

½ teaspoon black pepper

1. Set a grill/smoker to 225°F and add the wood chunks.

2. Combine all ingredients in a large mixing bowl and blend together. Transfer to an 8-inch aluminum pan and spread evenly.

3. Smoke for 20 to 30 minutes or until cheeses are melted thoroughly.

PRO TIPS

IN THE KITCHEN: Bake in the oven at 225°F for 20 to 30 minutes or until cheeses are melted thoroughly.

Serve with Burnt End Pork Belly Bites (page 46) and Griddled Donut BLD (page 28).

Enjoy the pimento cheese cold, spread on sandwich bread, as a good lunch.

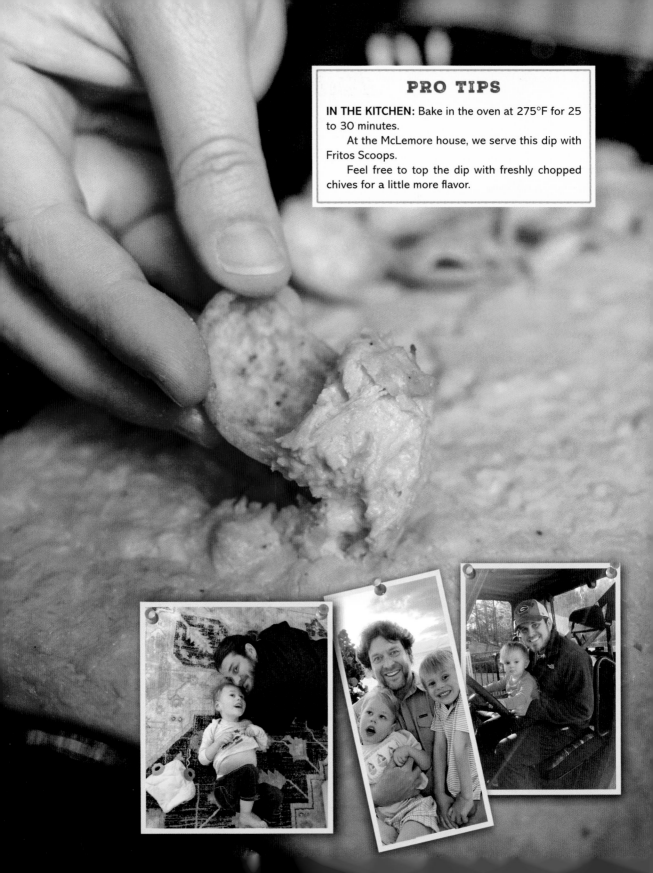

PRO TIPS

IN THE KITCHEN: Bake in the oven at 275°F for 25 to 30 minutes.

At the McLemore house, we serve this dip with Fritos Scoops.

Feel free to top the dip with freshly chopped chives for a little more flavor.

Brooke's Smoked Buffalo Dip

SERVES 8

The eldest daughter in the family, Brooke, got married on December 13, 2014 (12-13-14). Such a memorable date for sure, and it was a blessing to add her husband, Brian, to the family. Once Brooke started truly "adulting," this was her go-to addition to all family gatherings, and it's John II's favorite dip. Brooke's Buffalo dip has been the star of our parties for years. Not only is it delicious, but Brooke knows how to add that extra smoky flavor that takes it over the top.

And let's not forget Brooke and Brian's other new additions: Whit and Walt. We love having all of them around to keep us entertained—it never fails to create some hilarious moments and treasured memories, especially watching Whit eat some "ficy" Buffalo dip. For us, family gatherings are not just about the food but also the connections we make and the stories we share. Brooke's dip always adds that extra spark to our celebrations. Thanks for making us a Papa Mac and a Funcle John, Brookie—we love you!

Your favorite wood chunks (we recommend hickory)

2 (12.5-ounce) cans premium chunk white chicken, drained

1 cup cream cheese, softened

½ cup blue cheese dressing

½ cup hot sauce or wing sauce

½ cup shredded mozzarella cheese

1. Set a grill/smoker to 275°F and add the wood chunks.

2. In a large bowl, combine all the ingredients and mix together. Spread evenly in a 9 x 13-inch aluminum pan.

3. Smoke on the middle rack over indirect heat for 30 to 35 minutes, until the dip has an evenly melty consistency.

Bacon Pig Shots

SERVES 8

We're always looking for creative appetizers to impress *FOX & Friends* and their VIPs. For this recipe, we called on our friends and FOX hosts Rachel Campos-Duffy and her husband, Sean Duffy, to be our taste-testers. Rachel is always willing to try any of our crazy offerings and especially loves to take any leftovers home to their nine kiddos. They invited us to be on their podcast *From the Kitchen Table: The Duffys* and share our story. This appetizer is something extra special and unique just like they are! We created these savory, smoke-infused bites—and our VIPs were thrilled with the result. This recipe was a hit when we hosted another fantastic FOX summer concert and is guaranteed to be a crowd-pleaser at any party. So when you're looking for something special to please your guests, give these shots a shot. There's nothing quite like them!

1 pound kielbasa sausage, cut into 1-inch pieces

1 pound extra-thick-cut bacon, halved lengthwise

1 cup cream cheese, softened

1 cup sharp cheddar cheese

2 medium jalapeños, seeded and finely chopped

2 tablespoons sweet heat–style BBQ rub (we recommend Lane's BBQ Sweet Heat Rub/Seasoning)

1. Set a grill/smoker to 350°F.

2. Wrap the bacon strips around the kielbasa pieces with the bacon partially sticking up above the top of the sausage (this forms the "shot glass") and secure with a toothpick through the bottom to hold the bacon in place.

3. In a medium bowl, stir together the cream cheese, cheddar, jalapeños, and BBQ rub until well blended.

4. Spoon the cream cheese mixture into the bacon shot glasses, filling them to the top. Do not overfill the bacon cups, as the cream cheese mixture will puff up and ooze out as it cooks.

5. Smoke on the middle rack for 45 minutes to 1 hour, until the bacon is fully cooked and cheese is golden brown.

6. Remove from the smoker and let cool for a few minutes before removing the toothpicks.

7. Enjoy these shots with friends!

PRO TIPS

Place the cream cheese mixture into a 1-gallon zip-lock bag and cut a small piece off one corner of the bag to make a "redneck piping bag," then pipe the filling into the shot glasses.

Stir some of your favorite BBQ rub into the cream cheese mixture to add an extra kick of flavor.

Chris's Bacon-Wrapped Pickles

SERVES 6

Chris Patchin and his wife, Rhonda, have been our friends since 1996. Chris is a master of all things social media through his company Media Mule Marketing, but he's also a pretty good cook. We travel together quite a bit; he's usually with us at each FOX summer concert and at most of our cooking events. During our camping and tailgating trip to the Atlanta Motor Speedway in 2023, he showed us just how creative he can be at the grill. With just some pickles, bologna, and bacon, Chris created this uniquely flavored snack. Thank you, Chris, for being such an amazing friend and cooking up such a delicious recipe.

6 whole large dill pickles, halved lengthwise

12 slices bologna

1 pound bacon

BBQ rub (we recommend a brown sugar–based rub)

Alabama White Sauce (page 80)

1. Set a grill/smoker to 350°F.

2. Wrap each pickle half with 1 slice of bologna, then wrap in bacon over the bologna and secure with toothpicks. Season the outside of the bacon carefully with BBQ rub, being sure not to poke yourself with the toothpicks.

3. Place directly on the middle rack of the grill/smoker and place an aluminum pan underneath the bacon-wrapped pickles to catch the drippings. Smoke over indirect heat for 40 to 45 minutes, then move the pickles over direct heat for an additional 5 minutes to crisp the bacon.

4. Pull from the heat, drizzle with white sauce, remove toothpicks and serve.

PRO TIPS

Feel free to use a sweet-and-spicy BBQ rub to complement the saltiness of the pickle, bologna, and bacon if you don't want to use a brown sugar–based sweet rub.

Griddled Ham and Cheese Sliders

In our house, we all love a good ham sandwich. This variation on the classic is one of those sandwiches where after you take your first bite, you just can't help but smile. The mix of honey, mustard, mayo, sweet slider buns, Swiss cheese, ham, and poppy seed dressing all melted together is quite simply DADGUM good—and it all comes together with the help of a griddle. Whether we're camping in the woods or just grilling out on the back patio, this sandwich is always a hit. And it's easy to make! All you need are a hot griddle, a hungry family, and good friends.

⅓ cup yellow mustard

1 tablespoon honey

⅓ cup butter, melted

1 tablespoon poppy seeds

12 slider buns

12 slices deli ham

12 slices Swiss cheese

½ cup mayonnaise

1. Heat a griddle to medium.

2. In a small bowl, stir together the mustard and honey. Add the melted butter, then stir in the poppy seeds.

3. Split the buns sandwich-style, leaving the top and bottom attached at the hinge. Lightly coat the cut sides of the buns with the mustard mixture and griddle for 2 to 3 minutes, until toasted.

4. While the buns are toasting, place the ham directly on the griddle and top each slice with a slice of cheese. Cook until the cheese begins to melt, 3 to 4 minutes.

5. Spread mayo on the cut side of the slider buns.

6. When cheese begins to melt, place the ham and cheese inside the buns. Brush the bun tops with some of the mustard mixture and toast on the griddle for 3 to 5 minutes more. Serve and enjoy.

PRO TIPS

IN THE KITCHEN: Place on a baking sheet and bake in the oven at 350°F for 15 minutes, or until the cheese has melted and the buns are golden brown.

Burnt End Pork Belly Bites

At the Bass Pro Shops fiftieth anniversary celebration, we were asked to smoke up some pork belly for the crowd from the Bass Pro team using a unique Korean BBQ marinade. We weren't sure how that would turn out, as we don't have the luxury of such extended marinating times when we travel and cook for others and the Korean BBQ sauce was a new flavor to us. But we figured, why not give it a try? We added our smoke flavor to it, and boy, were we blown away! The longer it marinates, the better, so we recommend at least an overnight soak—and two or three days is even better. We love learning new techniques, and given how delicious this recipe turned out, we knew we had to share it with you. Turns out, you can teach an old dog some new tricks!

1 (8-pound) pork belly slab, trimmed and sliced into 1½-inch-thick strips

4 cups (32 ounces) Korean bulgogi BBQ sauce

Hickory wood chunks

1. Place the pork belly strips in a 1-gallon zip-lock bag and add two-thirds (about 3 cups/24 ounces) of the BBQ sauce. Seal the bag, place it in a pan in case it leaks, and refrigerate overnight.

2. Set a grill/smoker to 275°F.

3. Remove the meat from the marinade and place it on the middle rack of the grill/smoker. Cook over indirect heat for 3 hours, or until the internal temperature reaches 180°F.

4. Place a pan under the pork to catch drippings and pour the BBQ sauce from the bag over the pork.

5. Remove from the grill/smoker and cut into 1½-inch square pieces.

6. For crispy results, place the pieces on a griddle heated to high heat or in a cast-iron pan over high heat, coat with remaining sauce, and cook for 8 to 10 minutes, tossing frequently.

Smoked BBQ Nacho Bar

How many people can say that they camped in an RV in FOX Square in a snowstorm? Well, the McLemores did, and it was truly memorable! The only thing better than the experience was the amazing food we were able to serve for our FOX segment that day: a Smoked BBQ Nacho Bar! When it comes to tailgating (or homegating), you want to make sure the food is just as good, if not better, than what you'd get at the stadium. That's why our nacho bar has been a hit when we've served it at our events. We've traveled from Miami to Houston to the FOX Square in NYC—and no matter the venue, everyone has loved the nacho bar. Whether you're tailgating at the Super Bowl or just homegating with family and friends, this recipe will be sure to score big cheers with all your guests!

2 cups cubed Velveeta cheddar cheese

2 large bags tortilla chips

3 pounds pulled pork (see page 173), finely shredded

3 pounds pulled chicken (see page 180), finely shredded

3 pounds chopped brisket (see page 111), finely shredded

2 cups pickled jalapeños

2 cups banana peppers, sliced or chopped

2 cups mild salsa

2 cups sour cream

2 cups black olives, sliced

2 cups pico de gallo

2 cups refried beans

2 cups guacamole

2 cups chili

2 (8-ounce) bags shredded lettuce

2 cups of your favorite BBQ sauce

1 cup finely chopped green onions, for topping (optional)

1. Set a grill/smoker to 350°F.

2. Place the Velveeta in a heatproof bowl and place it in the smoker to melt for 15 to 20 minutes.

3. Cover your table with butcher paper and arrange the chips around the edges of the table.

4. Place the pulled pork, chicken, and brisket in the center of the table. Arrange the jalapeños, banana peppers, salsa, sour cream, olives, pico de gallo, refried beans, guacamole, chili, and lettuce around the meats.

5. Drizzle your nachos with the melted cheese and BBQ sauce and top with the green onions, if you like.

6. Serve to large crowd and enjoy!

PART 3
SIDES

Side dishes are what make a good meal complete and great. It's like pairing a good wine with a steak dinner; it's important to complement the meal with the right side. Steak and potatoes, BBQ and beans, shrimp and grits, and chicken and waffles. (Okay, we know waffles aren't a side, but they do complement the chicken well in this cookbook.) We hope these help you decide on the right side dish as you plan your next meal. And if you find yourself unsure about which side to pick, always opt for mac and cheese—it goes with absolutely everything.

Smoked Jalapeño Bacon Mac and Cheese

SERVES 8

This is the one recipe we *always* serve at our events and parties. From promoting the Masterbuilt smokers on QVC to serving it every week in New York for the FOX summer concert series, everyone loves our mac and cheese. We have smoked it, fried it, and served it on burgers and hot dogs. Once when we were at the Daytona 500 cooking for *FOX & Friends* with our buddy Rick Reichmuth, we even made mac and cheese patties and put them on the griddle. Rick is our friend and the founder of Weatherman Umbrella. He has been very instrumental in helping us get FOX segments on location everywhere from races to Super Bowls to holiday events in New York, as well as helping us get creative with cooking our mac and cheese. Come rain or shine, Rick has always been a great friend!

16 extra-thick-cut bacon strips (1 pound)

½ cup diced drained mild pickled jalapeños

1 teaspoon olive oil

1 (8-ounce) package elbow macaroni

½ cup shredded Velveeta cheese

4 cups shredded sharp cheddar cheese

1 cup sour cream

1 cup mayonnaise

2 teaspoons onion powder

1 teaspoon Cajun seasoning

Apple or hickory wood chunks

1. Set a grill/smoker to 275°F.

2. Cut the bacon into 1-inch squares and fry in a skillet (or on a griddle) over medium-high heat. As the bacon browns, add the jalapeños and cook until the bacon is crispy. Drain excess grease and set aside.

3. In a 4-quart pot, combine 8 cups water and the olive oil and bring to a rolling boil over high heat. Add the macaroni and boil for 8 to 10 minutes, until al dente, stirring every 2 minutes. Drain the macaroni and return it to the pot. While it's still hot, immediately fold in the cheeses, then mix in the bacon-jalapeño mixture, the sour cream, mayo, onion powder, and Cajun seasoning.

4. Transfer the mixture to a 9 x 13-inch aluminum pan and smoke on the middle rack for 1 hour, until all the cheeses are fully melted.

PRO TIPS

Fry extra bacon squares and add them to the top of the mac and cheese for extra flavor and presentation.

Double up on the jalapeños for extra kick.

Smoked Chili Lime Buttered Corn

SERVES 8

You know the scene in *Forrest Gump* when Bubba talks about cooking shrimp every way possible? That's how we feel about cooking corn. We love it smoked, grilled, boiled, fried, steamed, sautéed in a pan, from the cob or from a can, it doesn't matter—we simply love corn. So when we came up with the idea to smoke it in the husk with lime butter, it made the list!

Hickory wood chunks

6 to 12 ears corn, in their husks

1 to 2 sticks salted butter

Lane's BBQ Chili Lime Rub/
   Seasoning

1. Set a grill/smoker to 225°F and add the wood chunks.

2. Gently pulling back the cornhusks on each ear, but don't rip them off. Remove and discard the silk but leave the husks intact.

3. Place the corn, with the husks still pulled back in a large pot and fill with cold water to cover. Let soak for 2 hours, then drain the water and set corn aside.

4. In a microwave or small saucepan, melt the butter (use 1 stick for 6 ears corn, 2 sticks for 12) and add the chili lime seasoning.

5. With the husks still pulled back, brush each ear of corn with the chili lime butter, then pull the husks back over covering the corn kernels and tie the husks closed with kitchen twine.

6. Place the corn on the middle rack of the grill/smoker and cook for 2 hours.

7. Pull from the heat, remove the husks, and enjoy.

PRO TIPS

IN THE KITCHEN: Place the skillet in the oven and bake at 350°F for 30 minutes.

You can also use southwestern canned corn with poblano and red peppers, or Mexican-style canned corn, or even leftover grilled corn cut from the cob to give your version its own twist.

Street Corn

SERVES 8

We love making street corn anytime, anywhere. One of our most memorable times was at a campground in North Georgia during COVID. We were doing a Facebook Live event, sharing recipes, and corn kept getting stuck in our teeth. This is a great way to enjoy corn without having to floss it away afterward. You might start a new cherished recipe tradition that will be unforgettable as a side dish to your feast and adds a unique twist to your basic corn recipe. No matter where you serve this street corn recipe, it will always be "a-maize-ing."

6 cups (48 ounces) canned whole-kernel corn

½ stick salted butter

1 cup cream cheese

2 cups diced Gouda cheese

½ cup crumbled feta cheese

1 cup sour cream

½ cup mayonnaise

1 teaspoon kosher salt

1 teaspoon black pepper

1 teaspoon garlic powder

1 teaspoon chili powder

1 teaspoon paprika

1 teaspoon lime juice

Bacon bits (store-bought), for garnish

Fresh cilantro, for garnish (optional)

1. Set a grill/smoker to 350°F.

2. In a large cast-iron skillet, combine the corn and butter and sauté over medium-high heat for 8 to 10 minutes, until the corn starts to char lightly.

3. Add the cream cheese and let it melt, then fold in the Gouda and feta and stir to blend together.

4. Add the sour cream, mayo, salt, pepper, garlic powder, chili powder, paprika, and lime juice and stir well to blend together evenly.

5. Place skillet on the middle rack of the grill/smoker and cook for 30 minutes.

6. Remove and top with bacon bits and cilantro, if you like.

Cynthia's Smoked Sweet Potato Casserole

SERVES 8

Cynthia was John's seventh-grade art teacher and later became a part of the family when she married Pawpaw, the Ole Man, in 2016. Having taught the youngest of the McLemores, she definitely did not know what she was getting into, but she is now a treasured part of our family. She has an endearing laugh and is a competitive board game player. Every time we have a get-together at the house Cynthia always brings a dish to share. Sometimes it's a dessert and sometimes it's a side. No matter what it is, it's always good. We added a little smoke to her homemade sweet potato casserole, and she adds a little spice to Pawpaw's life. Thanks, Cynthia, and we love you.

PRO TIPS

IN THE KITCHEN: Bake in your oven at 350°F for 20 minutes instead of on your grill/smoker if you're staying inside for the day.

Make sure all the potatoes are around the same size so they'll cook evenly.

For the Casserole

Hickory wood chunks

Nonstick cooking spray

5 or 6 large sweet potatoes

Olive oil

1 cup (2 sticks) salted butter

1 cup granulated sugar

½ cup brown sugar

1 teaspoon vanilla extract

2 large eggs, beaten

½ cup heavy cream

For the Topping

⅓ cup butter, melted

1 cup brown sugar

⅓ cup all-purpose flour

⅓ cup pecans, finely chopped

1. Make the casserole: Set a grill/smoker to 350°F and add the wood chunks. Lightly grease a 9 x 13-inch baking dish with cooking spray.

2. Coat sweet potatoes with olive oil and smoke on the middle rack for 2 hours, or until fork-tender. Remove from the grill/smoker and set aside until cool enough to handle, then peel the potatoes and transfer the flesh to a bowl. Completely smash the sweet potato flesh.

3. Transfer the mashed sweet potatoes to a large pot and add the butter, granulated sugar, and brown sugar. Cook over medium heat until the mixture starts to bubble.

4. Remove from the heat and blend with a stick blender until creamy, then add the vanilla and let cool.

5. When the mixture is cool, add the eggs and cream and blend with the stick blender until well combined.

6. Pour the mixture into the prepared baking dish and place back on the middle rack in the grill/smoker. Cook at 350°F, uncovered, for 20 to 25 minutes.

7. Meanwhile, prepare the topping: In a large bowl, combine the melted butter, brown sugar, and flour and stir until all the butter has been absorbed. Add the pecans and stir.

8. Sprinkle the topping evenly over the sweet potatoes and return the baking dish to the grill/smoker. Bake, uncovered, for 30 minutes more.

PRO TIPS

IN THE KITCHEN: You can do this on your stovetop, but you won't get the delicious backyard smoked flavor you get by doing it on the grill/smoker.

You can serve these delicious potatoes with your favorite chicken or pork recipes!

Skillet Potatoes and Mushrooms

SERVES 8

Don McLemore, our family business veteran of forty years, came up with the perfect side dish for our Don's Cast-Iron Skillet Steak (page 98). He's an excellent cook himself and loves to experiment. After a little trial and error, he finally perfected this simple yet delicious recipe. It uses the same ingredients as his steak recipe—which saves time and money. Don's side dish is now an essential part of any steak dinner at our house. So if you want to impress your guests with a great steak dinner, don't forget our secret weapon—the Don McLemore special side dish! This spud's for you.

2 pounds golden potatoes

Extra-virgin olive oil, a dab

Kosher salt and black pepper

1 stick salted butter

6 garlic cloves, peeled

6 sprigs thyme, chopped

1 cup mushrooms, thinly sliced

1 small sweet onion, finely chopped

1. Set a grill to 450°F or on medium-high heat.

2. Cut the potatoes in half and coat with olive oil. Season with salt and pepper to taste, place in a large cast-iron skillet, and place the pan directly on the bottom rack to roast for 20 to 30 minutes, or until the potatoes are fork-tender.

3. Meanwhile, in a medium cast-iron skillet, combine the butter, half the garlic cloves, and thyme and place on the middle rack in the grill. Cook until the butter has melted, then add the mushrooms and onion and cook for about 20 minutes, stirring every 5 minutes.

4. Add the potatoes to the pan with the onion and mushrooms, including the remaining juice from the potatoes and cook for 20 minutes more.

5. Remove and serve with your favorite steak.

Smoked Twice-Baked Loaded Potatoes

SERVES 8

Smoke is a magical ingredient that transforms any food into something extraordinary. Take this potato and bacon dish, for example. It may seem simple, but when you add a hint of smokiness to it, everything comes alive! Suddenly, all the flavors blend together perfectly with a delectable topping of cheese, chives, bacon, and jalapeño—now *that's* what we call a real McLemore classic!

4 large russet potatoes

Extra-virgin olive oil

Kosher salt and black pepper

1 pound thick-cut bacon

½ cup pickled mild jalapeños, finely diced

1 cup whole or 2% milk

1 cup sour cream

1 stick salted butter

1 cup shredded sharp cheddar cheese

Fresh chopped chives, for garnish (optional)

1. Set a grill/smoker to 350°F.

2. Rinse the potatoes, pat dry, and place in a small tray (or leave in the sink for easier cleanup). Coat lightly with olive oil and season with salt and pepper to taste (we tend to go heavier on salt to help break down the potatoes). Place directly on the middle rack of the grill/smoker and cook for 2 hours, or until fork-tender.

3. Meanwhile, also smoke bacon strips until done—place pan below to catch drippings. Finely chop the bacon into bits and place in a bowl. Add the jalapeños and mix thoroughly.

4. Remove the potatoes and let cool, then cut each potato in half lengthwise and carefully scoop the flesh into a large bowl, being careful to leave some of the flesh attached to the skins to keep the potato skin shells intact.

5. Add the milk, sour cream, butter, and three-quarters of the bacon and jalapeños to the bowl with the potato flesh and mix well, smashing up all the potatoes.

6. Fill each potato skin shell with the potato mixture, dividing it evenly; it's okay if some are mounded up. Top with a layer of cheese (how much is completely up to you) and place the potatoes on the grill/smoker for 10 to 15 minutes to melt the cheese. Feel free to leave on to continue baking the cheese, you almost cannot overcook these.

7. Remove and top with chives and the remaining bacon-jalapeño mix. Enjoy!

PRO TIPS

Season the outside of your potatoes with your favorite salt-based BBQ rub prior to baking for an added layer of flavor.

PRO TIPS

IN THE KITCHEN: Mimi traditionally bakes her green bean casserole in the oven at 350°F for 1 hour, but we like to add that additional smoky backyard flavor by doing it on the smoker.

An easy way to elevate this dish is to sauté an 8-ounce package of sliced mushrooms in salted butter until soft; season with salt and pepper to taste, then add the mushrooms to the dish before smoking.

Mimi's Green Bean Casserole

SERVES 8

Shirley, also known as Mimi, is Tonya's mama. She has weathered a few tough life changes recently but is still smiling. In June of 2021, she lost her only son, Chris—Tonya's brother—to lung cancer, and lost her husband, Jon, six weeks later. Mimi is always full of energy and brings her flavor to all our gatherings; this casserole is normally her staple item. She never fails to bring a smile to our faces when we come together at family events, and her enthusiasm for our stories is infectious! We can always count on Mimi to give us her honest opinion with her trademark wit and humor. Thank you for being such an amazing part of our family, especially spending time with your great-grandbabies, Whit and Walt. You might not realize it, but your presence means so much to us ♥. Thanks for bringing your daughter into our lives.

6 (14.5-ounce) cans French-style green beans, drained

1 (8-ounce) block cream cheese, softened

1 (10.5-ounce) can cream of mushroom soup

½ cup sour cream

2 cups shredded cheddar cheese

1 (24-ounce) container fried onions

1. Set a grill/smoker to 350°F.

2. Place the green beans in a 9 x 13-inch aluminum pan. Add the cream cheese, soup, sour cream, and 1 cup of cheddar cheese and stir to combine.

3. Top with the remaining 1 cup of cheddar cheese and the fried onions and smoke over indirect heat for 1 hour.

4. Remove from smoker and serve.

Griddled Brussels Sprouts

SERVES 8

John II is a jack-of-all-trades who answers to many names: John, J-Mac, Gen 2, John Jr., Little John, and, of course, the classic Johnboy that his mom uses. John II is what most call him now, and how exciting is it for a father and son to be on such a cool journey together! He is a great cook himself and everyone knows he makes a mean steak or salmon dish. There are probably quite a few reasons to love him—but his cooking skills are definitely up there. So next time you're looking for a delicious meal, make sure you turn to one of the masters himself—John II! Everyone knows that these "little cabbages" are a great side, but done right, these are an unforgettable addition to your meal.

2 pounds Brussels sprouts, halved lengthwise

Olive oil

Kosher salt and black pepper

Garlic powder

Balsamic glaze

1. Heat a griddle to high.

2. Bring a large pot of water to a boil over high heat. Fill a bowl with ice and water and set it nearby. Add the Brussels sprouts to the boiling water and blanch for 2 minutes, then drain and submerge in the ice water to stop the cooking. Drain again.

3. Season the griddle with a dab of olive oil and salt, pepper, and garlic powder to taste. Add the Brussels sprouts to the griddle, cut-side down, and cook for 10 to 15 minutes, until golden brown. Feel free to add additional salt, pepper, and garlic powder to taste. In the last 2 minutes of cooking, drizzle the Brussels with balsamic glaze.

4. Transfer to a serving bowl and enjoy!

PRO TIPS

IN THE KITCHEN: You can easily do this recipe in a cast-iron skillet on the stovetop instead of on a griddle if the party is inside versus out in the backyard.

Drizzle with ranch dressing and add bacon bits at the end for the perfect additional pop.

Feel free to substitute a bourbon glaze for the balsamic glaze if you're not a fan of the balsamic flavor.

Brooke's Smoked Broccoli Casserole

SERVES 8

This broccoli casserole comes from Brooke, the eldest daughter in our family. She's completely mastered this recipe, and it's a given that it will be served at all family functions, showers, parties, and get-togethers. Brooke was a teacher for eight years and is now a pretty busy stay-at-home mama. She and her husband, Brian, have the blessing of raising two boys—Whit and Walt! Whit was seventeen months old when Walt was born on December 28, 2019, in a moment that changed all of their lives forever. Walt was brought back to life after being born not breathing and without a heartbeat. We truly thank God for the power of prayer and amazing doctors. Walt is a miracle of modern medicine. He has been diagnosed with a severe brain injury due to HIE (hypoxic ischemic encephalopathy) and cerebral palsy, is legally blind and deaf, and has a seizure disorder, but none of that has stopped him from living and loving every moment of life! He is our little miracle baby with a truly infectious smile and laugh. He has already taught us the value of

PRO TIPS

IN THE KITCHEN: Brooke also cooks this recipe in the oven, and you can easily do the same—just follow the same instructions.

Place the Ritz crackers in a 1-gallon zip-lock bag, seal the bag, and roll over the crackers with a rolling pin to crumble them.

To steam fresh broccoli, place in a steamer basket above boiling water in a covered pot for 5 to 6 minutes or until soft.

cherishing each day and laughing often. To learn more and follow Walt's journey, go to wonderfullymadewalt.com. This is a great but easy recipe for all those busy parents out there, as well as John II's favorite side, and is required at all of our functions.

2 bunches broccoli, cut into florets, or 4 cups frozen broccoli florets

1 (10.5-ounce) can cream of chicken soup

½ cup mayonnaise

½ cup sour cream

1 cup shredded cheddar cheese

1 large egg

1 teaspoon salt

1 sleeve, or 2 cups, Ritz crackers, crumbled

2 tablespoons butter, melted

1. Set a grill/smoker to 350°F.

2. Steam the broccoli for 5 minutes to soften. Feel free to steam according to packaging instructions. See Pro Tip.

3. In a large bowl, combine the broccoli, cream of chicken soup, mayo, sour cream, cheddar, egg, salt, and ¼ cup water. Transfer the mixture to a 9 x 13-inch aluminum pan.

4. Bake on the middle rack of the grill/smoker over indirect heat for 30 minutes. Remove from the heat, top evenly with the crackers, and drizzle with the melted butter. Return the pan to the grill/smoker to cook for a final 15 minutes, until the crackers have begun to turn golden brown and the cheese has fully melted.

Roasted Carrots with Brown Sugar and Honey

SERVES 8

Carrots are not just good for you—they can also be pretty tasty! Take them up a notch by grilling them with some brown sugar, honey, and butter. That sweet-and-savory combination is sure to have you coming back for more. It may not be the healthiest way to eat carrots, but trust us, it's worth trying at least once, maybe twice—even if the nutritionists won't "carrot all" (get it?!).

2 tablespoons honey, or to taste

¼ cup brown sugar

4 tablespoons (½ stick) salted butter, melted

1 tablespoon extra-virgin olive oil

Kosher salt

8 carrots, halved lengthwise and cut into 2-inch-long pieces

¼ cup fresh parsley, finely chopped

1. Set a grill to 400°F. Line a baking sheet with aluminum foil.

2. In a large bowl, combine the honey, brown sugar, melted butter, olive oil, and salt to taste. Lightly peel carrots to freshen and add to the bowl with honey mixture and toss to completely coat.

3. Place the carrots on the prepared baking sheet and spread them out evenly. Grill for 20 minutes, then flip and grill for another 20 minutes until fork tender.

4. Remove from the heat, top with the parsley, and enjoy!

PRO TIPS

Elevate this dish by wrapping your honey-coated carrots in bacon before grilling, then brush with leftover honey mixture after flipping.

PRO TIPS

IN THE KITCHEN: You can definitely do this in the kitchen using a slow cooker instead of a grill/smoker. Just combine all the ingredients in the slow cooker, cover, and cook on Low for 10 to 12 hours. Also, this recipe is even better the next day as leftovers.

Turnip Soup

Mickey Jones is a great friend of the McLemore family. He managed our Masterbuilt warehouse and facility with so much care and dedication, but most important, he always had our back when we needed him. Over the years, he's gifted us with many delicious homemade pound cakes and shared countless recipes. Mickey debuted this amazing turnip soup during the Christmas holidays at the McLemores'. We all agreed that it had to be in the book for everyone else to enjoy as much as we did. You can prepare this soup in a slow cooker or in a Dutch oven on the grill, which will bring that smoky flavor from the charcoal. We hope this true Southern comfort food will "turnip" at your house soon! Thank you, Mickey, for this instant classic. We cherish your friendship, golf outings with you, and your amazing food.

2 pounds Conecuh Sausage, cut into 1- to 2-inch pieces

3 cups chicken broth

2 (14.5-ounce) cans Ro-Tel diced tomatoes

1 (14.5-ounce) can black-eyed peas, drained and rinsed

1 (14.5-ounce) can navy beans, drained and rinsed

1 (14.5-ounce) can light red kidney beans, drained and rinsed

1 large yellow onion, chopped (optional)

1 large (27-ounce) can Margaret Holmes turnip greens

1. Set grill/smoker to 350°F.

2. In a large cast-iron Dutch oven, combine all the ingredients and mix together evenly. Bring to a boil on the stovetop over high heat, then cook for 5 minutes.

3. Transfer the pot to the middle rack of the grill/smoker and smoke for 3 to 4 hours, stirring occasionally.

Smoked BBQ Brunswick Stew

SERVES 12

We've got a family tradition: If we find ourselves in a new town, the first thing we do is look for the local BBQ restaurant and order some BBQ with Brunswick stew. We love to compare recipes, debate over secret ingredients, and try to one-up each other with our own versions. That was the original spirit behind this FOX summer concert series recipe: to bring a little bit of our family tradition to everyone attending as VIPs. Whether you're in New York watching a FOX concert and hanging out with us, or at home cooking up this stew in your backyard, we hope you enjoy it!

Your favorite wood chunks (we recommend apple wood)

2 tablespoons olive oil

1 cup diced onion

1 green bell pepper, diced

1 yellow bell pepper, diced

2 celery stalks, diced

1 tablespoon minced garlic

3 to 5 pounds Smoked Triple-Threat Pork Butt (page 173)

2 (12-ounce) cans diced tomatoes, with their juices

2 (12-ounce) cans cream-style corn

2 tablespoons hot sauce

2 tablespoons chili powder

2 teaspoons garlic powder

2 teaspoons BBQ rub

1 teaspoon kosher salt

1 teaspoon black pepper

1 cup sweet BBQ sauce

1 cup ketchup

Bread, for serving

1. Set a grill/smoker to 275°F and add the wood chunks.

2. In large pot, heat the olive oil over medium-high heat. Add the onion, bell peppers, celery, and garlic and sauté until soft.

3. Add the pulled pork, tomatoes with their juices, corn, hot sauce, chili powder, garlic powder, BBQ rub, salt, black pepper, BBQ sauce, and ketchup and stir to combine. Bring to a simmer and cook, stirring every few minutes, for 20 minutes. Remove from the heat.

4. Place on the middle rack of the grill/smoker and smoke, uncovered, over indirect heat for 2 to 3 hours, stirring every 30 minutes to blend flavors together.

5. Remove from the smoker and let cool. Serve with your favorite bread.

> ## PRO TIPS
> For a triple meat experience, also add in 1½ pounds of leftover chopped smoked brisket and 1½ pounds of leftover pulled smoked chicken!

T-Maw's Smoked Baked Beans

SERVES 8

The original matriarch of our family was MeMaw, so when Tonya became a grandmother, it was only natural that she became T-Maw. It's not hard to figure out why all the grandkids love T-Maw's baked beans . . . they are hands down the best! Every time we get together for a cookout or camping trip, you can count on T-Maw to whip up a delicious pan of this family favorite. From the first bite to the last bit of sauce, you know your taste buds are in for a treat. It's no surprise that we all hold T-Maw in such high regard, not only for her culinary skills, but also for the valuable family lessons we learn from her. Just like how food brings us together, so does our love and respect for T-Maw! She has taught us how to laugh, cry, live, love, share, and so much more.

Thanks, T-Maw/Mom/Tonya! We love you more than you will ever know.

Hickory wood chunks

3 (20-ounce) cans baked beans

½ cup yellow mustard

½ cup ketchup

¾ cup brown sugar

½ pound bacon, cut into strips

1. Set a grill/smoker to 350°F and add the wood chunks.

2. Place the beans in 9 x 13-inch aluminum pan and add the mustard, ketchup, and ½ cup of the brown sugar. Stir to combine, then top with the bacon strips. Sprinkle the bacon with the remaining ¼ cup brown sugar.

3. Place on the grill/smoker and smoke over indirect heat for 2 hours, or until the bacon is fully cooked.

PRO TIPS

IN THE KITCHEN: Bake in the oven at 350 degrees for 2 hours. We recommend cooking a little extra for leftovers, so good.

PART 4
SPICES, RUBS, AND SAUCES

Sauces and rubs are important for preparing great meals. Some people say that if a recipe is done right, you don't need a sauce. We agree with this, but we also love a good sauce to complement an already great dish. The right combination of spices and how they pair with certain meats can still be key for the recipe to be perfect. We have success at this because we have years of experience, but we also know the right people in the business. One of those experts is Ryan Lane of Lane's BBQ. He is a friend and someone who knows how to help give your recipes amazing flavor with his special blends. Not only do we use Lane's BBQ's exceptional sauces and rubs, we also create our own blends for something extra special. Our homemade recipes have a unique flavor that you won't find anywhere else. If you're looking to create a truly extraordinary meal while you Gather and Grill with great sauces, spices, and rubs, then be sure to try some of these.

Red Hot Sauce

1 stick salted butter

1 cup of your favorite hot sauce

1 cup ketchup

1 teaspoon garlic powder

Cajun seasoning

In a small saucepan, melt the butter over medium heat. Add the hot sauce, ketchup, garlic powder, and Cajun seasoning to taste and simmer, stirring every few minutes, for 15 minutes.

Alabama White Sauce

2 cups mayonnaise

1 cup apple cider vinegar

1½ teaspoons cayenne pepper

Kosher salt and black pepper

In small saucepan, combine the mayo, vinegar, cayenne, and salt and black pepper to taste and bring to a simmer over medium heat for 15 minutes, stirring every few minutes.

Blue Cheese Sauce

1 cup blue cheese dressing

½ cup hot sauce

¼ cup molasses

1 tablespoon minced garlic

1 teaspoon celery salt

1 teaspoon black pepper

In small saucepan, combine the dressing, hot sauce, molasses, garlic, celery salt, and pepper and bring to a simmer over medium heat for 15 minutes, stirring every few minutes.

DADGUM Good Espresso BBQ Sauce

2 tablespoons extra-virgin olive oil

2 tablespoons minced garlic

1 cup ketchup

1 cup honey

½ cup balsamic vinegar

¼ cup soy sauce

¼ cup espresso or strong brewed coffee

1. In a medium saucepan, combine the olive oil and garlic and cook over medium heat, stirring frequently, until golden, about 2 to 3 minutes. Remove from the heat and let the garlic cool in the oil.

2. Whisk in the ketchup, honey, vinegar, soy sauce, and espresso.

3. Return to medium heat and simmer for 15 minutes to blend the flavors.

4. Remove from the heat and serve warm.

Sweet-and-Spicy BBQ Sauce

2 cups ketchup

½ cup yellow mustard

½ cup packed brown sugar

¼ cup apple cider vinegar

2 tablespoons Worcestershire sauce

1 tablespoon liquid smoke

1 tablespoon red pepper flakes, to taste

1 tablespoon onion powder

1 tablespoon chili powder

1 tablespoon black pepper

2 teaspoons garlic powder

½ teaspoon celery salt

½ teaspoon kosher salt

1. Combine all the ingredients in a nonreactive medium saucepan.

2. Bring to a simmer over low heat, then cook, stirring occasionally, for 25 minutes, until smooth and thickened.

3. Let cool slightly and serve.

South Carolina BBQ Sauce

½ cup apple cider vinegar

6 tablespoons Dijon mustard

2 tablespoons honey

2 tablespoons ketchup

4 teaspoons Worcestershire sauce

1 tablespoon brown sugar

1 teaspoon hot red pepper sauce

2 teaspoons kosher salt

Black pepper

In a medium bowl, stir together the vinegar, mustard, honey, ketchup, Worcestershire, brown sugar, and hot sauce. Add the salt and black pepper to taste.

Come Back Sauce

1 cup Duke's mayonnaise

2 tablespoons red wine vinegar

1 teaspoon minced garlic

Kosher salt and black pepper

In a medium bowl, stir together the mayo, vinegar, and garlic. Season with salt and pepper to taste. Cover and refrigerate until ready to serve. The sauce will keep as long as mayo will stay good.

Creamy Mustard Sauce

⅓ cup mayonnaise

¼ cup sour cream

2 tablespoons Dijon mustard

1 tablespoon fresh lemon juice

In a medium bowl, stir together all the ingredients. Cover and refrigerate until ready to serve.

Whole-Grain Mustard Sauce

1 cup Duke's mayonnaise

½ cup maple syrup

2 tablespoons whole-grain mustard

1 tablespoon Dijon mustard

In a medium bowl, stir together all the ingredients. Cover and refrigerate until ready to serve.

DADGUM Good Seasoning

2½ tablespoons dark brown sugar

1 tablespoon paprika

1½ teaspoons light brown sugar

1 teaspoon lemon pepper

¾ teaspoon onion salt

½ teaspoon garlic powder

½ teaspoon celery salt

½ teaspoon ground ginger

½ teaspoon crushed dried sage

½ teaspoon cracked black peppercorns

¼ teaspoon ground marjoram—substitute for dried oregano

In a medium bowl, combine all the ingredients and mix thoroughly.

PRO TIPS

This seasoning is perfect for chicken, pork, or beef.

PART 5

MAINS

At the McLemores', we love sports, and we've played them all. We love how they all lead up to the end of the season, the main event. These recipes are great complements because they lead us to what we all look forward to the most in a meal: the main entrée. Whether we're on the road or just chillin' at home, we try to prepare what our guests love when we're gathering and grillin'. The MVP of The McLemore Boys' journey as we travel around the country is Halteman Family Meats, providing us with a wide selection of fresh meats. No matter what you serve as your favorite dish, we hope these mains will have you celebrating as if your family and friends just won the championship game, or at least so full and happy, you don't care.

For more information go to haltemanfamilymeats.com.

BEEF

POULTRY

PORK

FISH & SEAFOOD

WILD GAME

Reverse-Seared Tomahawk Steak

SERVES 4

This is definitely the coolest steak we cook and it always gets attention for its size, but also, and more importantly, for how it tastes. We have prepared this recipe in so many places—everywhere from cooking events for Super Bowls and races with the FOX team to the World Food Championships in Texas to the Flo Rida concert in 2022 at FOX Square in New York City—but no matter where we serve this masterpiece, it is always the star of the show. The steak is so DADGUM big and cool-looking that folks always want a picture of it—and we love fighting over who gets the bone!

Hickory wood chunks

1 (3-pound) bone-in
tomahawk steak

Extra-virgin olive oil, for brushing

Kosher salt and black pepper

Garlic powder

1. Set a grill/smoker to 225°F and add the wood chunks.

2. Brush the steak with a light coating of olive oil. Season with salt, then with pepper, then with garlic powder, and let sit at room temp for 30 minutes.

3. Smoke on the middle rack over indirect heat for 1 hour, or until the internal temp reaches 105° to 110°F.

4. Remove from heat and let rest for 15 minutes. Meanwhile, turn the grill up to 700°F or as hot as it can get.

5. Coat the steak again lightly with olive oil and place on the grill over direct heat to sear for 2 minutes each side, or until cooked to medium-rare.

6. Remove from the grill and cut the rib eye off the bone. Let rest for 10 minutes before slicing against the grain.

7. Season the bone and sear it for 2 minutes more.

8. Serve and enjoy. Be sure to let your guests fight over the bone!

Smoked French Cut Prime Rib

SERVES 8

Prime rib is typically what John II orders when we go out to a nice restaurant. Having someone prepare and serve it to you, along with a glass of your favorite red wine, can be nice. However, like most pitmasters, we prefer to cook our steaks ourselves at home. We might be a little bougie, but no one cooks it like we do. The secret lies in the smoke-infused flavor, the right amount of seasoning, and making sure it's cooked to the right internal temp. When we're making this recipe for guests, we always ask how they like their steak cooked. If anyone says well-done, we politely ask them to leave. Just kiddin'—we never invite them to begin with.

Your favorite wood chunks (we recommend hickory)

1 tablespoon black pepper

1 tablespoon white pepper

1 tablespoon garlic powder

1 tablespoon kosher salt

1 teaspoon paprika

1 teaspoon red pepper flakes

Onion powder

1 (5- to 6-pound) bone-in prime rib roast

1. Set a grill/smoker to 275°F and add the wood chunks.

2. In a large bowl, combine the black pepper, white pepper, garlic powder, salt, paprika, red pepper, and onion powder to taste.

3. Coat the prime rib roast on all sides with the spice rub and let sit at room temperature for 30 to 45 minutes.

4. Smoke on the middle rack with indirect heat for 30 minutes per pound, or to an internal temp of 125°F.

5. Remove from heat and let rest for 20 minutes before carving. (Carryover cooking should raise the internal temperature by 5 to 10 degrees to medium-rare doneness.)

6. Carve in between each bone and serve the steaks individually.

PRO TIPS

Once you carve each steak out in between each bone, re-season (optional) and sear at high temp (700 degrees) for 1 minute each side.

Seared and Braised Beef Chuck

Beef chuck is a cut of meat that can be tough if not prepared correctly. In this recipe, we keep the juices intact by searing before braising. This method helps keep everything tender without sacrificing flavor throughout the meat. The salt and beef broth also help tenderize and add to that bold flavor. How much wood could a woodchuck chuck if a woodchuck could chuck beef?

1 (4-pound) whole beef chuck

Kosher salt and black pepper

Garlic powder

Hickory wood chunks

4 cups (32 ounces) beef broth

6 garlic cloves, minced

1 large onion, chopped

1. Set grill to 700°F, or as hot as you can get it.

2. Season the beef lightly with salt, pepper, and garlic powder. Let sit at room temp for 30 minutes before cooking.

3. Sear for 5 minutes on each side. Pull off the grill and place in an aluminum pan.

4. Turn the grill down to 350°F and add the wood chunks.

5. Pour the broth into the pan with the chuck so the broth completely covers the meat (you may not need all the broth). Then cover with the garlic and onion, making sure some are on top of the chuck and the rest are scattered around it in the broth.

6. Grill, uncovered, for 3 hours, or until the internal temp reaches 200°F.

7. Serve and enjoy.

PRO TIPS

IN THE KITCHEN: Sear the chuck in a cast-iron pan on the stove over high heat for 5 minutes per side, then transfer to a slow cooker and add the onion, garlic, and enough broth to cover. Cover and cook on High for 6 hours.

Don's Cast-Iron Skillet Steak

SERVES 4

This recipe is special—not only because of the steak, but because of the family member we wrote it with, Don McLemore. Don was co-owner and COO of Masterbuilt from 1973 to 2012. He and John were partners in the family business from the time John was eight and Don was eleven, and they loved working together as brothers and best friends. When Don retired in 2012, he and John made a promise to each other to continue doing what they always did at Masterbuilt: cooking and making people happy. Don has always been the guy with the quick one-liners and can always make people laugh, so much so that at work, he was known as the COO—Comedic Opportunist Officer. Thanks, Don, for being a great partner, brother, uncle, and, most of all, best friend. We love ya, man!

2 (12- to 16-ounce) prime cut rib eye steaks (1½ inches thick)

Kosher salt and freshly ground black pepper

1 stick salted butter

6 sprigs thyme

6 garlic cloves, smashed and peeled

1. Set a grill to 450°F or on medium-high heat. Place a cast-iron skillet directly on the grill rack to preheat.

2. Season the steaks with salt first and then with pepper. Let sit at room temperature for 30 minutes while the grill is heating.

3. Put the butter in the hot skillet on the grill. When it has melted, add the thyme and garlic and stir together.

4. Place the steaks in the skillet and cook for 10 minutes, or until the internal temp reaches 100°F.

5. Remove the skillet from the grill, place the steaks in a separate pan, and let rest for 10 minutes.

6. Turn the grill up to 700°F or as hot as it can get.

7. Dredge the steaks in the butter mixture left in the skillet, then place them directly on the grill grates and sear for 1 minute per side, or until the internal temperature reaches 125°F.

8. Pull the steaks from the grill, let rest for an additional 10 minutes, then slice against the grain and serve.

PRO TIPS

For the perfect side, take a look at the potato, onion, and mushroom recipe on page 61.

When searing steak in a cast-iron skillet or on a griddle, use the following cooking times per side:

- 1 inch thick: 30 seconds
- 1½ inches thick: 1 minute
- 2 inches thick: 1½ minutes

Smoked Whole Beef Tenderloin

SERVES 8

We have had the privilege of meeting and sharing recipes with the former governor of Arkansas Mike Huckabee. We first met at FOX in 2010, and he kindly shared one of his own beef recipes with us. The most fun we ever had with this recipe was when he invited us to come cook on his TV show in Nashville and set up a competition against him. We added the sear technique to the process and won! We were a bit surprised by that, but were more surprised when he presented us with a brass pig with wings and told us that the only way we would ever get invited back to be on his show would be when pigs fly. We still have the flying pig, and we still have a great relationship that continues by sharing recipes with each other. Thanks, Governor.

Hickory wood chunks

1 whole beef tenderloin, trimmed

Kosher salt and black pepper

Garlic powder

Come Back Sauce (page 84), for serving

1. Set a grill/smoker to 225°F and add the wood chunks.

2. Season the tenderloin with salt first and then with pepper, then season liberally with garlic powder. Let sit at room temperature for 30 to 45 minutes.

3. Smoke for 1 hour, or until the internal temperature reaches 110°F.

4. Remove from heat and let rest for 15 to 20 minutes. Turn the grill/smoker up to 500°F.

5. Cut the tenderloin into thirds and sear for 2 minutes on each side.

6. Let rest for 5 to 10 minutes, then cut into ½-inch-thick slices and serve with Come Back Sauce.

PRO TIPS

Although more expensive, we prefer "trimmed" roasts from our local grocer or butcher over "untrimmed" roasts. The thick layer of fat on an untrimmed roast prevents the formation of that beautiful crust you get from the reverse sear. (PS: You can trim a roast yourself, but do not do it to save money—you'll easily trim off the savings, up to 3 pounds of meat.)

The lower the heat, the more evenly the roast cooks.

If you want the roast to cook at equal doneness from end to end, you must tie the tip under itself to create the same thickness as the butt end. However, if you're serving this at a dinner with guests who prefer different degrees of doneness, cook the roast as is. The tip will be on the well-done side and the butt will be the rarest.

Double Trouble Brisket/Butt Hoagie

SERVES AS MANY AS YOU WANT!

We're a big family—and we often cook for big crowds—so when we fire up the grill, we always have a ton of food. This sandwich idea came to us because brisket and Boston butt easily serves a lot of people. This was true when we had the pleasure of celebrating a first birthday in Austin, Texas, for Michael's son, Ben, the youngest member of our family. The joy of spending time with new extended family and building relationships is truly priceless.

At these events, we typically make sliders with one of the meats, but decided to combine the two meats and turn it into a big hearty sandwich that has all our favorite rubs and spices. When you add the meats and sauces with lettuce and a touch of banana peppers, it has people coming back for more.

PRO TIPS

Add your favorite cheese for another layer of flavor—we absolutely love sliced American cheese on this sandwich.

Favorite beef brisket, chopped

Favorite pulled pork, shredded

Large hoagie buns

Mayonnaise

South Carolina BBQ sauce

Chipotle sauce

Lettuce

Sliced banana peppers

1. Set a grill to 350°F. Toast the hoagie buns on the grill grates.

2. Warm up the brisket and pulled pork.

3. Build the hoagies by spreading mayo on the buns, then adding brisket slices and pulled pork. Finish with BBQ sauce and/or chipotle sauce, lettuce, and banana peppers to your preference.

Smoked BBQ Meatloaf Minis

SERVES 8

When you think of meatloaf, you either think of your grandma, or that small hole-in-the-wall local restaurant that serves it up with mashed potatoes and green beans. But we think of another FOX concert in New York City, when we served up these savory bites paired with mac and cheese for the VIPs while listening to Parmalee and Blanco Brown in FOX Square. We loved "Just the Way" every minute of it turned out—thanks, FOX!

Hickory wood chunks

2 cups finely chopped onion

2 cups finely chopped green bell pepper

2 teaspoons minced garlic

2 tablespoons extra-virgin olive oil

2 pounds lean ground beef

1 pound mild Italian sausage

1 cup Lane's BBQ Kinda Sweet BBQ sauce

1 cup fresh breadcrumbs

2 large eggs, lightly beaten

1 teaspoon kosher salt

1 teaspoon black pepper

½ teaspoon cayenne pepper

1 cup sweet BBQ sauce

1. Set a smoker to 275°F and add the wood chunks.

2. In a large pan or cast-iron skillet, combine the onion, bell pepper, garlic, and olive oil and sauté over medium heat until soft, 8 to 10 minutes. Remove from the heat and pour into a large bowl.

3. Add the beef, sausage, BBQ sauce, breadcrumbs, eggs, salt, black pepper, and cayenne to the bowl. Mix thoroughly to combine. Form the meat mixture into 4 small loaf-shaped logs.

4. Place the logs on the middle rack over a 9 x 13-inch aluminum pan to catch the drippings. Smoke for 2 hours, or until the internal temperature reaches 160°F. Lightly brush the top of each meatloaf with BBQ sauce every 30 minutes while smoking.

5. Remove from the smoker and let rest for at least 15 minutes before serving.

PRO TIPS

If you want your burger more well-done, flip and cook for an additional 2 to 3 minutes.

Griddled Smashed Mini Cheeseburger Sliders

SERVES 6

We have the privilege to meet some amazing people when we travel and cook at our events, but there is no greater honor than cooking for and serving food to members of our US Armed Forces. At FOX News on Memorial Day 2023, we served up these juicy burgers to honor our fallen soldiers. We served this burger to the hosts, all the VIPs, the band members of 3 Doors Down, and the sailors from the USS *Wasp*, which was docked in New York Harbor for Fleet Week. Nothing is more American than hamburgers. Good food becomes great food when it's served with family and friends as we remember those who made the ultimate sacrifice—it's why we love what we do, and hope we never take it for granted.

2 large eggs, beaten

2 tablespoons garlic powder

2 tablespoons onion powder

Kosher salt and black pepper

2 pounds 80/20 ground beef

2 tablespoons hot sauce

2 tablespoons mild steak sauce

Your favorite cheese slices (we recommend cheddar cheese)

1 pack slider buns

Duke's mayonnaise or Come Back Sauce (page 84)

Hamburger dill pickles

1. In a large bowl, combine the eggs, garlic powder, onion powder, and salt and pepper to taste. Add ground beef and mix..

2. Transfer the meat mixture to a 9 x 13-inch aluminum pan and flatten it evenly over the bottom. Cover with aluminum foil and refrigerate for 4 to 6 hours. (This helps the meat marinate for good flavor, but if time is limited, you can skip this step.)

3. Heat a griddle to medium-high.

4. Using a spatula, divide the meat evenly into 12 squares (each square will be a burger) while still in the pan and form each square into an individual ball roughly the same size as a golf ball (⅙ pound each).

5. Season the griddle with olive oil and salt.

6. In a small bowl, stir together the hot sauce and steak sauce.

7. Place each ball onto the griddle and smash it into a ½-inch-thick burger. Sear for 6 to 8 minutes total, flipping the burgers every 2 minutes, and don't forget to brush them with your sauce mixture!

8. Right at the end, add a thick layer of cheese to each burger (we like to double up the slices) and close the lid (if applicable). Cook until the cheese has melted.

9. Pull the burgers off the griddle. Build on slider buns with Come Back Sauce and top with pickles.

Bacon-Wrapped Cheeseburger Pizza Fatty

SERVES 6

Country music superstar Tyler Farr was performing at the 2023 FOX summer concert series in FOX Square while we served this recipe to all the VIPs. We're big fans of his music, and it was amazing to see how well he connected with the crowd. We had fun with him backstage, talking about all the people we knew together back home, and how there's nothing much better than good ole boys like us who love to hunt, fish, eat, and listen to good music. If you love cheeseburgers and pizza, and listening to really great music with your friends, you will absolutely be "Redneck Crazy" for this recipe, and for Tyler Farr.

1 pound thick-cut bacon

1 pound ground beef

1 pound ground sausage

2 teaspoons kosher salt

1 teaspoon dried basil

1 teaspoon dried oregano

1 teaspoon paprika

1 teaspoon garlic powder

1 teaspoon onion powder

1 teaspoon black pepper

2 tablespoons pizza sauce

2 ounces black olives, drained (¼ cup)

1 cup shredded mozzarella cheese

1 cup sliced mushrooms, sautéed

½ pound thinly sliced pepperoni

1. Set a grill/smoker to 250°F.

2. Create a bacon weave on waxed paper (see the box on p. 110) and set aside.

3. In a large bowl, combine the beef, sausage, and all seasonings and mix thoroughly, then place the meat mixture in a 1-gallon ziplock bag and seal, removing as much air as possible from the bag. Flatten out the meat in the bag, patting it into a layer of equal thickness throughout.

4. Using a knife, cut the bag open at the seams on each side, but keep the bag underneath the meat to make transportation easier later on.

5. Spread the pizza sauce over your meat sheet just like you are making a pizza. Then add the olives, some of the mozzarella, the mushrooms, pepperoni, and more mozzarella in the center.

PRO TIPS

If your smoker will only heat to a max of 275°F, simply keep the meatloaf on the smoker longer to reach 165°F.

Fill this fatty with your favorite toppings. If you're not a mushroom and olive lover, try peppers and onions or pineapple and ham. This is another one of our recipes where the options are endless!

6. Use the bottom of the bag to help roll the meat into a loaf. Seal the ends of the loaf and the ends wrapped up to the top to prevent the filling from oozing out.

7. Roll the meatloaf onto your bacon weave, using the waxed paper to wrap the bacon weave around the meatloaf.

8. Place the meatloaf on the middle rack of the grill/smoker and smoke for 2 to 3 hours, until the internal temperature reaches 145°F.

9. Increase the grill/smoker temp to 400°F and cook for about 1 hour more, until the internal temp reaches 165°F.

10. Remove the meatloaf from the smoker and let rest for 15 minutes before cutting into 1-inch-thick slices.

11. Serve and enjoy with a side of pizza sauce.

FOR A BACON WEAVE: On a work surface, lay half the slices of bacon parallel to each other. Fold every other piece back and lay one of the remaining slices down perpendicular to the slices lying flat. Unfold the slices and then fold back the opposite pieces. Continue until you have an entire sheet of woven bacon.

3-Step Beef Brisket

This is another recipe inspired by collaboration with our great friend Ryan Lane, the owner of Lane's BBQ. Ryan was a big help to us for all the FOX concert series in New York because brisket is a staple on our menus. We not only learned how to perfect our brisket with Lane's seasonings, but how to get creative with so many other things to do with brisket. No matter how you serve this 3-step brisket—Griddled Donut BLD (page 28), Double Trouble Brisket/Butt Hoagie (page 102), or on the best leftover Smoked Brisket Sandwich ever (page 220)—it is always a huge success. Thanks, Ryan Lane and Lane's BBQ!

Cherry wood chunks

1 (12- to 15-pound) whole packer-style beef brisket, untrimmed

¼ cup kosher salt, plus more as needed

¼ cup black pepper, plus more as needed

¼ cup garlic powder, plus more as needed

We recommend using Lane's BBQ SPG Rub/Seasoning in place of the individual seasonings.

1. Set a grill/smoker to 225°F and add the wood chunks.

2. We recommend not trimming brisket, but if you do, trim it lightly, leaving at least ½ inch of fat. See Pro Tip.

3. Place the brisket in a large aluminum pan and season liberally with the salt, pepper, and garlic powder. Feel free to go heavy with the seasoning, and do not leave any exposed areas on the brisket.

4. Place the brisket fat-side up on the middle rack of the grill/smoker and place a pan below the brisket for indirect heat and to catch drippings. Smoke for 1 hour per pound, or until the internal temp reaches 180°F.

5. Pull the brisket from the heat, wrap it at least twice with butcher paper and then a layer of heavy-duty aluminum foil, keeping it fat-side up.

6. Put the brisket back on the smoker for 2 to 3 hours more to bring the internal temp up to 202°F.

7. Remove the brisket and place it, still wrapped, into an empty cooler to rest for 2 hours before slicing. Do not skip this step! Keeping the meat wrapped and letting it rest are the keys to this recipe.

8. Unwrap the brisket and thinly slice it against the grain, then serve.

PRO TIPS

If you trim, only trim the hard thick fat off and cook with fat cap up.

Pink butcher paper is recommended, and always put the waxed side facing the meat.

When buying your brisket, look for a good fat cap and marbling. The brisket should be flexible when held in the middle.

For quicker results, set the grill/smoker to 275°F and smoke for 6 to 8 hours, or until the internal temp reaches 180°F. Wrap and continue to smoke until the internal temp reaches 200° to 205°F. Pull and remember to let rest for 2 to 3 hours before slicing.

A brisket is made up of two parts, the point and the flat. When cooking a whole brisket (both the point and the flat), make sure to separate them after cooking before slicing. The grain on each section runs in the opposite direction of the other.

Seared Skirt Steak Tacos with Corn Salsa and Chimichurri

SERVES 4

We cooked up this awesome recipe in New York for the 2022 FOX summer concert series. We knew we wanted to serve steak, but having it on the menu for one hundred VIPs and all the FOX crew was going to be a challenge. The solution? Skirt steak, taco-style. This recipe is easy and fun to make—and especially good for a crowd. Best paired with good music! FOX cohost Carley Shimkus happens to be a passionate taco connoisseur. Her incredible smile and fun personality bring a special kind of energy to these events, and her enthusiasm for tacos is even more infectious. We'll definitely be bringing out skirt steak tacos again soon—after all, a good taco needs the perfect taste-tester! Thanks for always being there, Carley.

For the Corn Salsa

- 3 cups raw sweet corn kernels (from about 4 cobs)
- ½ medium red onion, finely chopped (1 cup)
- 1 ripe avocado, diced (optional)
- ½ cup finely chopped fresh cilantro (from about 1 bunch)
- 2 to 3 medium jalapeños, finely chopped (use 2 for mild to medium spiciness, 3 for spicier salsa)
- ¼ cup fresh lime juice (from about 2 limes), to taste
- 1 tablespoon red wine vinegar
- ¼ teaspoon chili powder

Skirt Steak Tacos Instructions:

1. Make the corn salsa: Mix all the ingredients together in a large bowl, cover with aluminum foil, and refrigerate for a minimum of 2 hours until serving.

2. Make the chimichurri: In a medium bowl, combine the parsley, olive oil, chile, garlic, vinegar, salt, black pepper, and 1 to 2 teaspoons Lane's SPF53 Rub. Mix well. Cover and refrigerate for up to 24 hours before serving.

3. Make the steak tacos: Set a grill to high heat or 600°F.

4. Dry the skirt steak with paper towels and coat both sides lightly with olive oil. Season with salt and pepper (we recommend being liberal with the salt).

For the Chimichurri

1 cup fresh flat-leaf parsley, finely chopped

1 cup extra-virgin olive oil

1 small red chile, seeded and diced

4 garlic cloves, peeled and minced

2 tablespoons red wine vinegar

1 teaspoon kosher salt

1 teaspoon black pepper

Lane's SPF53 Rub

For the Skirt Steak Tacos

1 pound skirt steak

Extra-virgin olive oil

8 small soft taco shells

Kosher salt and black pepper

5. Sear for 1 to 2 minutes on each side, until the internal temp reaches 120°F. For this recipe, the more medium-rare, the better, so be sure to not overcook the meat.

6. Remove and let rest for at least 5 minutes before cutting into thin slices against the grain (the thinner, the better).

7. To serve, place a couple of slices of steak in the center of a taco shell. Add a light layer of the corn salsa and then top with some chimichurri. Roll up and enjoy.

PRO TIPS

IN THE KITCHEN: You can sear the skirt steak in a cast-iron skillet on the stovetop over high heat if you want to stay in the kitchen for this recipe!

Feel free to add as much or as little of the corn salsa and chimichurri as your taste buds prefer. We find that after your first taco, you can adjust the amounts to your desired perfection!

Double Bacon and Cheddar Smash Burger

SERVES 4

At a charity event in Atlanta a few years ago, we had the opportunity to judge a burger contest, and we ended up testing twenty different burgers. Getting through that many burgers was fun and challenging, but worth it—we learned a lot from trying such a wide variety of burger styles and techniques. This recipe combines some of the best tricks we learned that day. It's a fun and challenging recipe, but just like that contest, it's also well worth it. Any time you smash a burger, add bacon, and stack on a second burger, lettuce, and tomato, get ready to get messy. It may not be twenty burgers, but it's close to it.

2 pounds 80/20 ground beef

2 large eggs, beaten

1 tablespoon Lanes BBQ Sweet Heat BBQ rub

¼ cup tomato-based BBQ sauce

8 slices cheddar cheese

1 pound bacon, halved lengthwise

4 large hamburger buns

Duke's mayonnaise

1 large tomato, sliced

1 head lettuce

Kosher salt and black pepper

1. Heat a griddle to high.

2. In a large bowl, combine the ground beef, eggs, and BBQ rub and mix evenly. Form the meat mixture into eight 4-ounce balls.

3. Place the balls on the griddle and smash them with a spatula. Cook for 5 minutes, flip, and brush with BBQ sauce. Cook for 5 minutes more, or until the burgers reach medium doneness. Place the cheese slices on burgers for the last two minutes to melt the cheese.

4. Cut bacon in half lengthwise and make a 3 x 3 weave. Cook alongside the burgers to the desired crispiness.

5. Toast the buns on the griddle until golden brown.

6. To build the burgers, spread the buns with mayo, add your first burger, then a mini bacon weave, followed by a second burger, tomato, lettuce, and finally salt and pepper to taste.

PRO TIPS

Chop half the bacon before cooking and add it to the raw hamburger mixture for another level of flavor.

Brian's Seared New York Strip

SERVES 4

Since Brian joined our family, we've learned that his ability to sear a steak on his Kamado-style grill at crazy-hot temperatures is as good as they come. It was only fitting for us to ask him for a recipe that was his go-to meal, and steak was what he chose. Brian's family owns a local HVAC business called Climate Control here in our hometown. He runs the business with his father, Ronnie Trevathan, and they're the hardest-working fellas we know. It's great to share the journey of owning a family business with another father and son. Thanks, Brian, for being a great addition to the McLemore family and a good cook!

2 (16-ounce) New York strip steaks

Kosher salt and black pepper

Garlic powder

4 tablespoons (½ stick) salted butter, melted

¼ cup panko breadcrumbs

¼ cup shredded Monterey Jack cheese

1 tablespoon sugar

¼ cup sour cream

¼ cup Duke's mayonnaise

1 tablespoon sriracha

1. Set a grill to 700°F or as hot as it can get.

2. Season the steaks with salt, pepper, and garlic powder to taste and let sit at room temperature for 10 to 15 minutes.

3. Sear the steaks for 1 minute per side. Remove and let rest for 10 minutes.

4. While the steak is resting, in a small bowl, mix the melted butter, panko, cheese, and sugar until evenly combined.

5. Cut the steak into ½-inch-thick slices and place in a cast-iron skillet, but keep the pieces lined up together.

6. Cover the steak slices with the butter mixture and put the skillet directly on the grill grate. Cook at 350°F for 10 to 20 minutes, until the steak reaches medium-rare doneness.

7. Mix together sour cream, mayo, and sriracha for a creamy sauce to top the steak with.

Smoked and Seared Bologna Sandwich

SERVES 8

Pan-fried bologna sandwiches with mustard have always been a favorite at the McLemores'. Tonya pan fries a round slice of bologna on the stovetop, and toasts the bread, just for us. Because we love bologna so much, we decided to share the smoked version that we make for larger crowds. When you add smoke flavor throughout and that burnt edge on the outside, then top it with melted cheese and a tomato, you realize that this is not just another typical bologna sandwich.

Hickory wood chunks

1 (2½-pound) log bologna

½ cup yellow mustard

DADGUM Good Seasoning (page 87)

16 slices provolone cheese, plus more for topping

8 potato buns or sandwich buns

Duke's mayonnaise

2 large tomatoes

1. Set a grill/smoker to 275°F and add the wood chunks.

2. Score the bologna with 1-inch squares, ¼ inch deep, making roughly 8 cuts in either direction; it should look like a checkerboard.

3. Lightly coat the bologna with mustard and season liberally with DADGUM Good Seasoning.

4. Smoke on the middle rack with indirect heat for 4 hours.

5. Remove and slice the bologna into 8 slices along the scored lines (the goal is for these to be 1-inch slices).

6. Add 2 slices of cheese to each piece of bologna and put them back on the middle rack of the grill. Cook until the cheese melts, 2 to 3 minutes.

7. Toast the bread on the grill and then spread it with mayo and mustard (your preference on amount). Add the bologna slices and top with cheese and tomato. Cut the sandwiches in half, if desired, and enjoy!

PRO TIPS

Dry brining is a method of brining without any liquid to make your meat as juicy as possible. The salt crystals must be larger than those of table salt to dry brine, which is why we recommend kosher salt or coarse sea salt.

Smoked Beef Ribs

SERVES 6

Lawrence Jones loves to eat with us when we come to NYC or when we travel with FOX to cook. Ribs were on the menu when we were all at the Talledega race and this rib recipe was a good surprise for the FOX team. When we think of ribs, we typically think of pork ribs. But when we want a change from the typical, we don't want the cow to feel left out from the pig, so we make Fred Flintstone–style beef ribs and Lawrence gave us his approval. We think they may even make you say "Yabba-Dabba-Doo!"

1 large 3-bone-in beef ribs

1 cup kosher salt or coarse sea salt, or more as needed to cover the ribs

Hickory wood chunks

Worcestershire sauce

2 cups apple juice

1. To dry brine the ribs, pat them dry with a paper towel, place in a pan, and season liberally on all sides with the salt. Cover with aluminum foil and refrigerate for a minimum of 4 hours or overnight.

2. Remove the ribs from the refrigerator and let stand at room temperature for 1 hour.

3. Set a grill/smoker to 275°F and add the wood chunks.

4. Wipe excess salt from the ribs and lightly coat them with Worcestershire.

5. Smoke on the grill/smoker on the middle rack with indirect heat for 5 hours, or until the internal temperature reaches 180°F. Spritz with apple juice every hour to add flavor and keep the meat moist.

6. Remove and double wrap with heavy-duty foil.

7. Turn the grill up to 450°F and place the ribs back on the middle rack. Cook for 1 hour more, until the internal temperature reaches 200°F.

PRO TIPS

Be sure to say your meal prayer and give MeMaw a toast before diving in. We salute you, MeMaw, and miss you bunches.

MeMaw's Southern Fried Chicken

SERVES 4

This recipe—and the story behind it—is near and dear to the whole McLemore family. Evelyn (Boots) McLemore, known as MeMaw to all the kids, was the backbone of our family and a strong Christian woman of faith. This is the only recipe that has been repeated in every cookbook we've written and will continue to be as we go forward. It's not because the fried chicken is the best (although it is) but because the woman who always made it for us was the best. MeMaw and the Ole Man were happily married for fifty wonderful years. She instilled values in us all that will stay with us forever, and taught us never to complain and to always be thankful as we go through life. She prayed for us every day and asked God to protect us. She held our family together and expected us to put family first. She was beautiful inside and out and saw the good in everyone. She was an amazing cook and will always be remembered by everyone who had the privilege of knowing her. Thanks, MeMaw, for always watching out for us.

2 gallons peanut oil, for frying

1 cup buttermilk

1 cup self-rising flour

1 fryer chicken (about 4 pounds), cut into individual pieces

1 teaspoon kosher salt

1 teaspoon black pepper

1. Fill a deep fryer with the oil (we recommend the Masterbuilt electric fryer) and heat to 375°F.

2. Place the buttermilk and flour in two separate bowls.

3. Season the chicken pieces with the salt and pepper. Dip each piece in the buttermilk and then dredge in the flour to completely coat.

4. Carefully place the dredged chicken in the hot oil and deep-fry for 15 minutes, until the chicken is golden brown and the internal temperature reaches 165°F. Remove from oil and serve hot.

Smoked Bloody Mary Start-Your-Engine Wings

At the 2023 Daytona 500, we cooked for the *FOX & Friends* weekend crew. Cohost Joey Jones was a gamer and excited to give our wings a try so early in the morning. This race is always a big party, so we came up with this recipe because we figured that a lot of people would need help as they woke up each morning that weekend. It's been said that Bloody Marys are a great hangover cure, so we marinated some wings with the iconic drink for all the race fans. As we started cooking at 5 a.m. for the FOX cooking segments, people who hadn't been to bed yet from the night before would come by, so these wings were perfect.

For the Wings

5 to 6 pounds chicken wings

2 tablespoons extra-virgin olive oil

Lane's BBQ Honey Sriracha Rub/Seasoning

4 cups tomato juice

1 cup vodka

1 cup brown sugar

½ cup hot sauce (we recommend Lane's BBQ One Legged Chicken Buffalo Sauce)

2 tablespoons prepared horseradish

1 tablespoon Worcestershire sauce

Kosher salt and black pepper

Juice of 2 lemons (½ cup)

1. Make the wings: Divide the wings between two 9 x 13-inch aluminum pans. Coat the wings with olive oil and season with honey sriracha seasoning.

2. In large bowl, combine the tomato juice, vodka, brown sugar, hot sauce, horseradish, Worcestershire, salt and pepper, and lemon juice. Whisk until fully blended.

3. Pour the tomato juice mixture over the wings until they are fully submerged, reserving one-third; set the remainder aside in a small saucepan. Cover the pans with aluminum foil and marinate in the refrigerator for at least 1 hour or up to overnight.

4. Set a smoker to 275°F. Remove the wings from the pans and place on smoker for 45 minutes to 1 hour.

5. Meanwhile, bring the remaining tomato juice mixture to a simmer over medium heat. Cook for 20 minutes or until thickened.

6. Make the dip: In a small bowl, stir together the sour cream, horseradish, and dill. Cover and refrigerate until ready to serve.

PRO TIPS

For crispier burnt end results, place the wings directly on the grill grate for 5 to 6 minutes and get them to an internal temp of 120°F.

For the Dip

1 cup sour cream

1 tablespoon prepared horseradish

1 tablespoon chopped fresh dill

7. Place the wings back in a 9 x 13-inch pans and coat with the thickened sauce. Place back on the grill to bake at 350°F for 20 to 25 minutes, or until the internal temperature reaches at least 180°F.

8. Serve the wings with the dip alongside.

PRO TIPS

Use two spatulas and cook the pile of wings like you would cook fried rice on a hibachi grill, tossing them every 2 to 3 minutes. You can use this technique whether you're searing on a grill or a griddle.

If you have a griddle handy, you can use it to sear the wings over high heat with the remaining steak marinade for amazing burnt end results! Definitely recommended!

Smoked 'n' Seared Burnt End Wings

One of John II's favorite things to cook and eat are wings, which means that wings are on the menu at most of the events we do. Whether we're at a FOX summer concert hanging out with Gavin DeGraw's band while serving the VIPs, at the Super Bowl events with FOX, or at home watching a game or a race, we cook a lot of wings. This recipe ranks as one of our best because the wings are *smoked and seared*. This gives them a unique, moist flavor and the crisp burnt ends that we all love. "You can't beat eating the perfect wing right off the grill after getting to cook them like rice with two spatulas," as John II will say sometimes. No matter where you are or who you're hanging out with, these wings are sure to please.

6 pounds chicken wings

2 cups low-sodium thick steak marinade (we recommend Dale's Seasoning Reduced Sodium Blend)

Apple wood chunks

Kosher salt and black pepper

1. Place the wings in a 9 x 13-inch aluminum pan and cover completely with half the marinade (use more if needed). Cover with aluminum foil and refrigerate for a minimum of 2 to 4 hours. The longer you marinate the wings, the saltier they will be!

2. Set a grill/smoker to 250°F and add the wood chunks.

3. Place the wings directly on the middle rack of the grill/smoker and cook for 45 minutes. Discard marinade and place pan below wings. Remove wings from the smoker and raise the temp to 500°F.

4. Toss the wings with the remaining marinade in a new pan.

5. Place the wings directly on the bottom rack of the grill/smoker, sprinkle with salt and pepper to taste, and sear for 10 to 15 minutes, turning them every 2 to 3 minutes, until they reach your desired burnt end crispiness.

Patriotic Red, White, and Blue Wings

SERVES 8

We love wings, and we love our country. These three sauces represent our nation's colors and satisfy a good number of taste buds. We served this wing recipe at the 2020 FOX Super Bowl event in Miami, as well as for our brave men and women of our military during a Lee Brice concert in Fort Hood, Texas. Wings are always a great appetizer for parties at home or for tailgating at your favorite event. So, if you love hot sauce (red), a traditional Alabama white sauce (white), or blue cheese (blue), these sauces hit the spot every time.

Apple wood chunks

6 pounds chicken wings

¼ cup kosher salt, plus more if needed

¼ cup black pepper, plus more if needed

Red Hot Sauce (page 80), Alabama White Sauce (page 80), or Blue Cheese Sauce (page 80)

1. Set a grill/smoker to 275°F and add the wood chunks.

2. Season the wings with the salt and pepper (feel free to add more, if preferred).

3. Smoke the wings on the middle rack with indirect heat for 1 hour, or until the internal temp reaches 160°F.

4. Remove the wings from the smoker and place them in 3 separate aluminum pans. Coat with your choice of red, white, or blue sauce (do not mix sauces), saving half the sauce for dipping.

5. Put the wings back on the grill or in the oven at 400°F for 15 minutes, or until the internal temp reaches 180 to 200°F.

6. Serve with the remaining sauce alongside for dipping.

PRO TIPS

If you want extra done and crispy wings, remove them from the pan and sear them on a hot grill direct for 3 to 5 minutes; using two spatulas, flip them like you would rice on a griddle.

Sweet-and-Spicy Wings

SERVES 8

We are honored to have this wing recipe representing The McLemore Boys in Carley's cookbook, *Cooking with Friends!* If you love your wings a little sweet and a little spicy, this recipe is for you. Combining all the rubs with smoke-infused flavor and then honey with hot BBQ sauce just simply takes this wing recipe to another level. What we love about cooking wings is how forgiving they are, especially when they're drizzled with honey BBQ sauce—enjoy!

Apple wood chunks

2 tablespoons black pepper

1 tablespoon kosher salt

1 tablespoon garlic powder

1 tablespoon onion powder

1 tablespoon chili powder

6 pounds chicken wings

1 cup honey

1 cup hot BBQ sauce

¼ cup apple juice

1. Set a grill/smoker to 250°F and add the wood chunks.

2. Mix all dry seasonings together and completely coat all wings and let sit for 30 minutes.

3. Place wings on indirect heat, smoke for 1 hour or until 165°F internal temp.

4. In a saucepan, blend together honey, BBQ sauce, and apple juice on low heat.

5. Remove wings and place in 9 x 13-inch aluminum pan, then drizzle with the honey BBQ blend.

6. Place back on the grill/smoker and cook at 350°F until the internal temp reaches 180 to 200°F.

Chicken Lollipops with Sweet Chili Sauce

SERVES 8

Kids love lollipops and kids love chicken. So, why not give them what they want and combine the two, like we so often do? This is a recipe that takes a bit of work and is a labor of love to prepare. But our kids are worth it, and the adults love it, too. The work on the front end makes enjoying the chicken leg on the back end so worth it, especially given the sweet chili sauce that it's cooked in . . . INSANE FLAVOR!

2 cups sweet chili sauce

¼ cup extra-virgin olive oil

¼ cup teriyaki sauce

2 tablespoons lemon juice

1 teaspoon kosher salt

1 teaspoon black pepper

16 large chicken legs

1. In a large bowl, stir together the sweet chili sauce, olive oil, teriyaki, lemon juice, salt, and pepper until evenly combined.

2. Cut the skin and tendon of each chicken leg just above the knuckle and remove the skin and tendon to expose the bone, using a paper towel for better grip.

3. Place the legs in a 1-gallon zip-lock bag and pour in three-quarters of the sweet chili marinade. Seal the bag, removing any air pockets, and put it in a pan in case the bag leaks. Refrigerate for at least 2 hours, or overnight for best flavor.

4. Set a grill/smoker to 350°F.

5. Grill the chicken legs over direct heat for 30 minutes, or until the internal temperature reaches 160°F, rotating them every 10 minutes.

6. Remove and place in aluminum pan. Pour the remaining sweet chili marinade over the chicken.

7. Place the chicken legs directly on the bottom grill grates and cook for 15 minutes more, or until the internal temp reaches 180°F.

PRO TIPS

Be sure to remove all the extra *junk* from the chicken leg above the knuckle and below the meaty part of the leg. This is what creates the lollipop effect and helps make the leg more tender when you eat it. It will literally fall off the bone when cooked to 180°F. Plus, it looks super cool!

PRO TIPS

Pull the turkey out of the oil and let rest for a minimum of 5 minutes before checking the internal temp—checking it too soon right out of the hot oil can give you an inaccurate reading.

Deep-Fried Buffalo Ranch Turkey

SERVES 12

Our family business, Masterbuilt, has a reputation of being innovators. For us, R and D stood for "research and develop," not "research and duplicate." We looked for problems in the outdoor cooking world and worked hard to solve them. In 2002, we developed the "World's First Indoor Electric Turkey Fryer." Everyone loved deep-frying turkey but was scared of burning their house down in the process. This product solved that problem and allowed people to safely fry a turkey and boil and steam whatever they wanted in one product. It was so popular that we traveled the country showing it off on TV, talking about it on the radio, and doing interviews with all the top magazines to tell our story. We had fun promoting something that had never been done before—and frying turkeys everywhere. From on set at FOX News with all our favorite hosts to on Sean Hannity's radio show at Radio City Music Hall and in houses across America, we gave people the peace of mind to enjoy frying their turkeys without the danger.

3 gallons neutral oil (we recommend peanut oil), for frying

8 ounces dry ranch seasoning

Meat syringe

1 (12- to 16-pound) turkey, completely thawed if frozen

Kosher salt and black pepper

1½ cups ranch dressing

1½ cups hot sauce

1. Fill a deep fryer with the oil (we recommend the Masterbuilt electric fryer) and heat to 375°F. (Be sure to follow the manufacturer's instructions and respect the capacity limitations of your fryer.)

2. In a small bowl, stir together the dry ranch seasoning and 2 cups hot water. Using a syringe, inject the ranch mixture into all parts of the turkey.

3. Season the outside of the turkey with salt, pepper, and the remaining dry ranch seasoning.

4. Carefully place the turkey in the hot oil and fry for 4 minutes per pound according to the packaged weight, or until the internal temperature in the meatiest part of the breast reaches 160°F.

5. Carefully remove the turkey from the oil and set aside to drain on a bed of paper towels and rest for 15 minutes.

6. In a small bowl, mix the ranch dressing and hot sauce together.

7. Carve the turkey and drizzle with the ranch hot sauce.

Smoked Honey Pecan Glazed Turkey Breast

SERVES 6

If you want to impress your family and guests at Thanksgiving and Christmas, this is the turkey recipe for you. But it's so good, why wait until the holidays? The honey glaze also works great poured over chicken, ribs, or even a scoop of vanilla ice cream—yep, ice cream. At the McLemores', we will try anything once, and if we like it, we do it again and invite friends over to share.

Apple wood chunks

1 (4- to 6-pound) bone-in turkey breast, ribs and back removed

Extra-virgin olive oil

Kosher salt and black pepper

Cajun seasoning

1 cup honey

1 cup chopped pecans

4 tablespoons (½ stick) salted butter

1. Set a grill/smoker to 275°F and add the wood chunks.

2. Coat the turkey breast with a light layer of olive oil, then season with salt, pepper, and Cajun seasoning to taste. (Some like their turkey saltier and spicier, and some don't!)

3. Smoke the turkey for 30 minutes per pound based on the packaged weight or until the internal temperature in the meatiest part of a breast reaches 160°F.

4. While the turkey is smoking, in a small saucepan, combine the honey, pecans, and butter and heat over medium heat, stirring continuously to prevent the bottom of the pan from burning. Remove from the heat and let rest for 15 minutes before carving.

5. Place the turkey breast on a serving tray and pour over the honey glaze, then carve to serve.

Smoked/Grilled Spatchcocked Turkey

SERVES 12

Master Chef Tony Seta is in a select group of world-renowned chefs who trained at the American Culinary Federation. Tony was also the executive chef for Butterball when we owned Masterbuilt, and we worked together for many years, developing recipes, doing a few cooking videos, and cooking together at corporate events for our companies. Tony always had a way of teaching us techniques to prepare food without making us feel like he was any smarter—even though he is when it comes to food. More important, he's a true friend. We learned this technique years ago from Master Chef Tony, and it's still one of the best ways to cook turkey or chicken.

1 (12- to 16-pound) turkey, completely thawed if frozen

Extra-virgin olive oil

Lane's BBQ Signature Brine mix

Apple wood chunks

Lane's BBQ SPG Rub/ Seasoning (or substitute salt, black pepper, and garlic powder)

Apple cider vinegar or apple juice, for spritzing

1. To spatchcock the turkey, place it breast-side down on your cutting board. Cut along the right side of the backbone from the tail to the neck, then cut along the left side to remove the backbone completely. Flip the bird over and break the breastbone by pressing down on the wings, flattening out the bird.

2. Coat the turkey liberally with olive oil and season on both sides, inside and out, with the brine mix. Do not leave any spots exposed. Follow the brining instructions on the package.

3. Set a grill/smoker to 350°F and add the wood chunks.

4. Remove the turkey from the brine, pat dry with a paper towel, and then cover all sides with SPG.

5. Place the turkey on the middle rack of the grill, breast-side up, laying it completely flat over direct heat, and cook for 2 to 2½ hours, spritzing with vinegar every 15 minutes, until the internal temperature in the meatiest part of the breast reaches 165°F. Do not block the heat below the turkey. The cooking time will vary depending on the size of your turkey.

6. Remove and let rest for 15 minutes, carve, and serve hot for best results!

PRO TIPS

For crispier skin, flip the turkey breast-side down and place it directly on the bottom grill grates for the last 30 minutes of cooking.

PRO TIPS

We like brining in alcohol because the alcohol binds to both fat and water molecules, adding depth of flavor to your dish. Beer also contains enzymes that break down the fibers in meat, making it more tender. And we recommend buying a few extra beers . . . you get the point. CHEERS!

Smoked Spatchcocked Chicken

Back in the day, MeMaw would always buy whole chickens and cut them up herself to save money. As The McLemore Boys grew up, we learned to cut up our chickens like MeMaw did. But when it came time to smoke or grill chicken, we learned years ago how to spatchcock our birds from our friend Tony Seta. Master Chef Tony showed us that we can use the same process for chickens that we use for turkeys (see page 142) when smoking/grilling, which makes this a budget-friendly recipe but also a cool way to cook a whole chicken.

1 whole 4- to 5-pound chicken

2 beers (we recommend a standard light-style beer)

Extra-virgin olive oil

Kosher salt and black pepper

Lane's BBQ Sweet Heat Rub/ Seasoning

1. Place the chicken in a 1-gallon zip-lock bag. Pour in the beers and seal the bag, making sure to remove all air from the bag. Place the bag in a pan in case the bag leaks and refrigerate overnight.

2. Set a grill/smoker to 400°F.

3. Remove the chicken from the fridge and drain the beer from the bag into a separate bowl or container; set the beer aside.

4. To spatchcock the chicken, place it breast-side down on your cutting board. Cut along the right side of the backbone from the tail to the neck, then cut along the left side to remove the backbone completely. Flip chicken over and break the breastbone by pressing down on the wings, flattening out the bird.

5. Coat the chicken liberally with olive oil and season on both sides, first with salt, then pepper, and finally with Sweet Heat rub, making sure to cover the entire chicken.

6. Place the chicken flat on the middle rack, breast-side up. Place an aluminum pan in the smoker underneath the chicken and pour the leftover beer into the pan. Smoke for 1 to 2 hours, until the internal temperature at the meatiest part of the breast reaches 155°F.

7. Pull and let rest for at least 10 minutes before serving; carryover cooking should raise the internal temp to 165°F.

Griddled Chicken Fajitas

SERVES 6

Chicken fajitas are great to serve at parties. Both kids and adults love them, they're perfect for a big crowd, and they're quick and easy to serve. We love preparing them on the grill or griddle to serve up hot. If you want to get a little creative, take your chicken and all the toppings and create a fun fajita bar for your family and friends, especially the kiddos!

4 boneless skinless
   chicken breasts

Extra-virgin olive oil

1 tablespoon kosher salt

1. Set griddle to medium heat temperature.

2. In a 9 x 13-inch aluminum pan, add chicken and coat with olive oil.

PRO TIPS

You can swap out the chicken in this recipe for steak, shrimp, or portobello mushrooms, or use all 4—we love variety!

1 teaspoon black pepper

1 teaspoon red pepper flakes

½ teaspoon ground cumin

1 red bell pepper, thinly sliced

1 yellow bell pepper, thinly sliced

1 green bell pepper, thinly sliced

1 large onion, thinly sliced

12 large tortillas, warmed, for serving

1 large bag shredded fiesta blend cheese

Alabama White Sauce (page 80)

Lime wedges, for serving

3. In a separate bowl, add all dry ingredients and mix to create seasoning. Add seasoning to all sides of chicken.

4. Add chicken to griddle and sear chicken for 5 minutes on each side, or until the internal temp reaches 160°F. Remove from the heat and slice into ½-inch nuggets.

5. Add olive oil, peppers, and onions to the griddle and sear for 8 to 10 minutes, seasoning to taste with salt and pepper.

6. Mix sliced chicken in with peppers and onions on griddle and cook for 8 to 10 minutes.

7. Place tortillas shells on griddle for 1 to 2 minutes to warm.

8. Pull shell and load with all ingredients and drizzle with the white sauce, hold with toothpick if desired.

Good Ole Boy Chicken Thighs

SERVES 6

Ain't nothing better than a big meal after a hard day's work on a tractor at the hunting land with good ole boys who love to eat. Chicken thighs are one of our favorite things to cook after these kinds of days. They're super filling, extremely forgiving, and, thanks to the bone in the thigh, always bursting with flavor.

This recipe comes from our farm manager and great friend, Sam Tedders. Sam is one of those guys who can do just about anything when it comes to hunting, fishing, plowing a field, and even cooking one of our recipes. He's like the Dos Equis guy—one of the most interesting men you will ever meet. We've learned so much from working with him on our farms, so we wanted to repay the favor by including Sam's spin on one of our favorite chicken thigh recipes. Happy hunting, fishing, farming, and eating—thanks, Sam!

12 bone-in chicken thighs

2 cups Italian salad dressing

Lane's BBQ Honey Sriracha Rub/Seasoning

1. Place the chicken thighs in a 1-gallon zip-lock bag and pour in 1½ cups of the Italian dressing. Seal the bag and place it in a pan in case it leaks. Refrigerate a minimum of 4 hours or overnight (recommended).

2. Set a grill/smoker to 275°F.

3. Place the chicken thighs on the middle rack of the grill/smoker, skin-side down, and sprinkle with the rub/seasoning to taste. Cook for 2 hours, or until the internal temperature reaches 160°F. Every 30 minutes, brush the thighs with some of the remaining Italian dressing.

4. Pull the chicken thighs off the grill/smoker and let rest for 10 minutes. Turn the grill to 500°F or high heat.

5. Place the thighs skin-side up over direct heat and sear for 5 minutes, then flip and sear for 5 minutes more, until the skin is crisp and the internal temperature reaches 180°F.

6. Pull and let rest for 5 minutes, then enjoy!

Grilled Boneless Chicken Thighs

SERVES 4

While at FOX for one of the concerts, weekday host Brian Kilmead asked for a simple chicken recipe. One thing people may not know about John is that one of his go-to personal recipes is a boneless chicken thigh—the reason is, it's cheaper and a lot more forgiving on the internal temperature than other parts of the chicken. We especially like this recipe because it's super easy to make and takes very little time. We may not be able to get him to eat on air, but (we assume) he has tried this at home. Happy eating, Brian!

8 boneless, skinless
  chicken thighs

Black pepper

Garlic powder

½ cup Worcestershire sauce

½ cup teriyaki sauce

1. Season the thighs with pepper and garlic powder on both sides. Put the thighs in a 1-gallon zip-lock bag.

2. In a small bowl, stir together the Worcestershire and teriyaki sauces until evenly combined, then pour into the bag with the chicken. Seal the bag and place it in a pan in case it leaks. Refrigerate for a minimum of 2 hours, or overnight for best results.

3. Set a grill to 450°F or medium-high heat.

4. Grill the chicken thighs for 5 to 6 minutes on each side, or until the internal temperature reaches 180°F. Remove from the heat and enjoy!

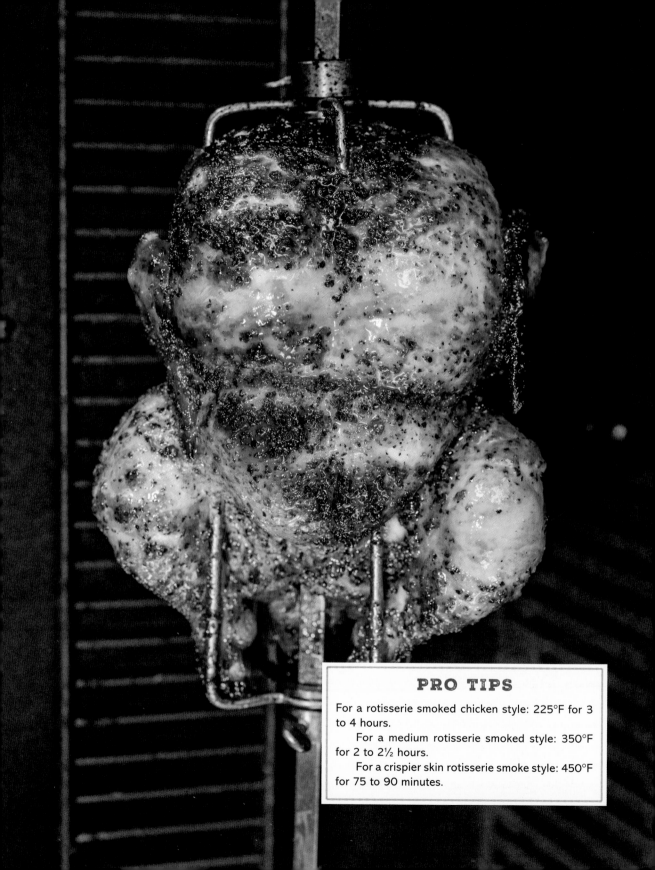

PRO TIPS

For a rotisserie smoked chicken style: 225°F for 3 to 4 hours.

For a medium rotisserie smoked style: 350°F for 2 to 2½ hours.

For a crispier skin rotisserie smoke style: 450°F for 75 to 90 minutes.

Rotisserie Lemon Pepper–
Brined Chicken

SERVES 4

We first cooked this recipe in New York at the 2023 FOX summer concert with country music duo LoCash in mind. For a big crowd, we had to use a large cooler to hold more chickens and pack it with ice water overnight for the brine! It was an awesome day feeding the concert VIPs and hanging with friends, new and old. Brining is a great way to infuse flavor into your meat and helps get juicy results throughout the whole chicken. This lemon pepper brine is so easy and packs lots of flavor inside and out. Whether you smoke or grill your chicken or turkey, brining will help you get tender, juicy, flavorful results every time. It'll really make you really "Love This Life"!

1 whole 4- to 5-pound chicken

1 cup lemon pepper seasoning, plus extra for rubbing

2 cups (16 ounces) apple juice

1. Place the chicken in a 2-gallon zip-lock bag. Add the lemon pepper seasoning and 8 cups cold water to the bag and seal. Massage the bag to evenly mix all the seasoning within, then place the bag in a pan in case it leaks. Refrigerate for at least 1 to 2 days, or 3 days for optimal results.

2. Set a grill/smoker to 450°F and set up grill with rotisserie.

3. Remove the chicken from the bag and place it in a 9 x 13-inch aluminum pan; do not rinse it first. Pour the brine from the bag over the chicken and rub in the extra lemon pepper seasoning.

4. Tie the chicken legs and wings so they'll stay in place on the rotisserie. Place the chicken on the spit rod of a rotisserie and secure both ends. Rotisserie for 75 to 90 minutes, spritzing with apple juice every 15 minutes, until the internal temp at the meatiest part of the breast reaches 155°F.

5. Remove the chicken on the spit rod from the grill and let rest until the internal temp reaches 165°F.

6. Remove from the spit rod, carve, and serve.

PRO TIPS

If you're waiting on guests to arrive, wait to reverse sear the sliders so you can serve them warm and juicy. We love these sliders because they are a great cost-effective way to serve a crowd.

Reverse-Seared Pork Tenderloin Sliders

SERVES 8

We make this recipe all the time when we're on the road, traveling for events, or hosting parties at the McLemore house. The beauty of sliders lies in their versatility—they can be made from any type of meat, and they always please a crowd. Pork tenderloin is a great cut of meat because it's quick on the grill and each tender slice fits perfectly on a slider bun with some Come Back Sauce. Top it off with a pickle for that extra touch of flavor.

½ cup brown sugar

2 tablespoons kosher salt

1 tablespoon garlic powder

1 tablespoon onion powder

1 teaspoon chili powder

1 teaspoon paprika

2 (1½- to 2-pound) pork tenderloins

16 slider buns

Come Back Sauce (page 84)

1 (32-ounce) jar sliced hamburger dill pickles

1. Set a grill/smoker to 225°F.

2. In a small bowl, combine the brown sugar, salt, garlic powder, onion powder, chili powder, and paprika. Season the tenderloins on all sides with the seasoning mix.

3. Smoke the pork on the middle rack for 30 to 45 minutes, or until the internal temperature reaches 120°F.

4. Pull the tenderloins off the grill/smoker and let rest. Turn the grill up to 600°F or high heat.

5. Return the pork to the grill/smoker and sear for 2 to 3 minutes per side, or until the internal temp reaches 145°F. Let rest for 10 minutes before slicing.

6. Slice the tenderloins crosswise into ½-inch-thick rounds and serve on the buns, with some Come Back Sauce and a pickle.

Bone-in Rotisserie Pork Roast

SERVES 8

At the FOX summer concert series in 2023, we had the pleasure of cooking for country music stars Justin Moore and Riley Green. It was the weekend of Father's Day, so it was especially cool for us because we had family in from Texas, Michael and Jana Spooner, to hang out with us in New York. We were able to share our recent McLemore family story about welcoming Michael, John's new-found forty-year-old son and John II's new older brother, as the newest addition to The McLemore Boys crew. If you want to impress Dad and show off to your friends, this is the perfect recipe to prepare. Anything cooked over an open fire on a rotisserie for all the dads will turn out great.

1 large (8 bones) bone-in pork loin rib roast

½ cup brown sugar

¼ cup kosher salt

¼ cup of your favorite BBQ seasoning

2 tablespoons garlic powder

1 tablespoon black pepper

2 cups (16 ounces) apple juice

1. Set a grill to 450°F.

2. Lightly trim excess fat off the pork roast.

3. In a small bowl, mix together the brown sugar, salt, BBQ seasoning, garlic powder, and black pepper. Season all sides of the pork roast with the seasoning mix.

4. Push the spit rod from a rotisserie directly through the center of the roast and lock in both claws. Place the rotisserie on the grill over direct heat and cook for 75 to 90 minutes, or until the internal temp reaches 145°F, spritzing the roast with apple juice every 15 minutes.

5. Remove the rotisserie from the grill and let the pork rest for 15 minutes before cutting it into individual chops. Serve and enjoy.

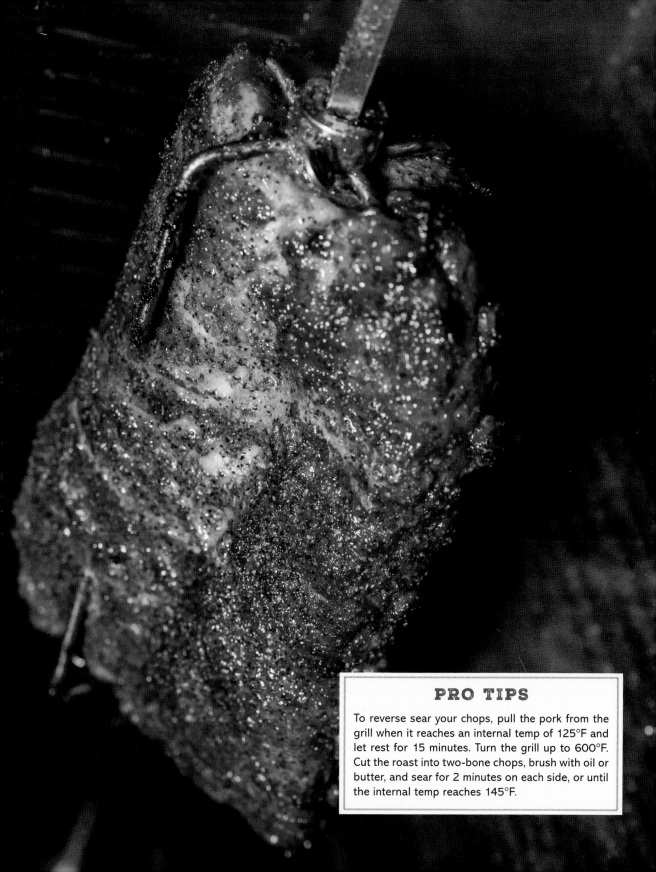

PRO TIPS

To reverse sear your chops, pull the pork from the grill when it reaches an internal temp of 125°F and let rest for 15 minutes. Turn the grill up to 600°F. Cut the roast into two-bone chops, brush with oil or butter, and sear for 2 minutes on each side, or until the internal temp reaches 145°F.

Grilled Pork Tenderloin with Black Pepper Honey

SERVES 8

One of our favorite parts of our job is traveling the world and cooking with amazing chefs from all different places. We learned this super "complicated" recipe from one of those fancy chefs . . . that's so easy everyone can do it. This pork recipe fits well no matter where we go—everyone is drawn to the black pepper honey. It's such a unique flavor of sweet and savory, and whenever we've served it, whether at the many events we did during our Masterbuilt days or on family camping trips, everyone's loved it. We know you will too!

1 cup pure honey

1 tablespoon black pepper, plus more as needed

Kosher salt

Garlic powder

Brown sugar

2 (1½- to 2-pound) pork tenderloins

1. Set a grill/smoker to 350°F.

2. In a small bowl, stir together the honey and pepper and chill until ready to serve.

3. In a separate small bowl, stir together salt, pepper, garlic powder, and brown sugar to taste. Liberally season the pork on all sides with the seasoning mix.

4. Grill the pork for 15 minutes per side (30 minutes total), or until the internal temp reaches 145°F. Pull the pork off the grill and let rest for 5 to 10 minutes.

5. Cut the pork into ½-inch-thick slices and serve drizzled with the black pepper honey sauce or with the sauce alongside for dipping. Enjoy!

PRO TIPS

You can also serve this with Come Back Sauce (page 84).

Pork Loin

SERVES 12

When feeding a crowd at an event or party (like we do most every week), buying meat at a good price is important. Whole pork loin works well for us because we can buy it at a reasonable price per pound and serve it to the masses. It's also great because we can smoke it before the event or party starts and then reverse sear it to serve hot. It's great served as an entrée or sliced and put on a slider bun to feed more people.

1 (8- to 10-pound) whole boneless pork loin

DADGUM Good Seasoning (page 87)

1. Set a grill/smoker to 225°F.

2. Place the pork loin in a pan (for easy cleanup) and liberally season the entire loin with DADGUM Good Seasoning.

3. Place the pork on the middle rack and smoke for 2 hours, or until the internal temp reaches 125° to 130°F. Pull and let rest for 20 minutes. Turn the grill up to 600°F.

4. Cut the loin in half right through the middle and then cut each half in half again lengthwise. Season all sides of the smaller loins.

5. Place the pork on the grill, cut-side down, and sear for 2 to 3 minutes, or until the internal temp reaches 145°F.

6. Remove and let rest for 15 minutes, then cut into ½-inch-thick slices and enjoy.

PRO TIPS

After carving the pork loin, let it sit on the cutting board in its own juices for even more flavor.

FOX & Friends Traditional Smoked Ribs

SERVES 4

We call this recipe "*FOX & Friends* Ribs" because we cook and serve it a lot for the hosts and crew at FOX News. We also call it that because Whit, Brooke's eldest son, became a star at FOX for eating these ribs. On a family camping trip in the North Georgia mountains, we made these ribs and served them up. Whit, two years old at the time, got his hands on one and would not let it go. He loved this rib so much, he showed all of us how to gnaw down, using both hands and tuning out everything around him. We grabbed the camera and filmed the whole thing, and *FOX & Friends* aired the video the next week!

Apple wood chunks

2 slabs pork spareribs

Your favorite BBQ rub (we recommend our DADGUM Good Seasoning, page 87)

South Carolina BBQ Sauce (page 83)

Apple juice, for spritzing

1. Set a grill/smoker to 200°F and add the wood chunks.

2. Prep the ribs by pulling the membrane off the back side. Season the ribs liberally with BBQ rub.

3. Place them on the middle rack in the grill/smoker. For easy cleanup, place an aluminum pan below the ribs to catch the drippings. Smoke for 3 hours, spritzing with apple juice every 30 minutes.

4. Remove the ribs and place on sheet of aluminum foil. Coat with BBQ sauce and double wrap with foil.

5. Place the ribs back on the middle rack and smoke for 2 hours.

6. Remove the ribs from the grill and turn the grill up to 300°F. Unwrap the foil, place the ribs in a pan, and coat again with BBQ sauce.

7. Return the ribs to the grill and cook for 1 hour more to caramelize the BBQ sauce. Serve and enjoy!

PRO TIPS

To start peeling the membrane from the ribs, use a butter knife and wedge it right in the middle of the rack and once you've got it started, grip the membrane with a paper towel and remove it. The membrane will be too slippery to pull off the rack with just your fingers.

60-Minute Grilled Ribs

SERVES 4

We all love slow-smoked ribs—not only because they taste so good, but because the process of making them is really fun. One day, we were planning to cook ribs for dinner but stayed on the boat too long to have them ready in time. So we said, "Let's do burgers," but our crowd said, "No, we will wait for the ribs!" Instead of smoking them as we normally would, we fired up the grill and cooked them over direct heat so we could eat dinner on time. Well, we were pleasantly surprised at how good they were. Not fall-off-the-bone, but moist, tender, full of flavor, and crazy delicious. If you're pressed for time, these are a great way to do ribs within an hour. Now we're sometimes late on purpose just to have an excuse to make these ribs again!

2 slabs baby back pork ribs

Lane's BBQ Spellbound Rub/ Seasoning or your favorite steak seasoning

BBQ sauce (we prefer Lane's BBQ Southbound Sauce; optional)

1. Set a grill/smoker to 375°F.

2. Remove the membrane from the back of the ribs. Season liberally with the seasoning.

3. Place the ribs on the grill, meat-side up, and cook, flipping every 15 minutes, for 1 hour, or until the internal temp is 145°F.

4. If you like, brush the ribs with your favorite BBQ sauce and smoke for 15 minutes more.

5. Remove from the grill, cut the slabs into individual ribs, and enjoy.

Smoked Honey-Glazed Spareribs

SERVES 4

For the July 4 segment at the 2023 FOX summer concert and for *FOX & Friends*'s weekend segment, we presented the crew with a 4½-foot-tall rib tree. Each rib was served with mashed potatoes and gravy, mac and cheese, and a rib to use as a fork. Practical, no . . . fun and worth sharing, absolutely! If you're looking for a way to build a rib buffet, this is how you do it.

Apple wood chunks

2 slabs St. Louis–style spareribs

Lane's BBQ Sweet Heat Rub/Seasoning

½ cup liquid butter, or 1 stick salted butter, melted

1 cup brown sugar

½ cup honey

Lane's BBQ Pineapple Chipotle sauce

1. Set a grill/smoker to 225°F and add the wood chunks.

2. Pull the membrane off the back side of the ribs. Season both sides liberally with Sweet Heat rub.

3. Smoke the ribs on the middle rack over indirect heat for 2 hours.

4. Remove from the grill/smoker and place on a sheet of aluminum foil. Top the ribs liberally with the butter, then with the brown sugar and honey. Double wrap in foil.

5. Place the wrapped ribs back on the middle rack of the grill/smoker and cook at 225°F for 1 hour more.

6. Remove the ribs from the smoker and turn the grill/smoker (or griddle, if you have one) up to 500°F (or high heat, if using a griddle).

7. Unwrap the ribs and cut the slabs into individual ribs. Place the individual ribs in an aluminum pan and brush BBQ sauce on each rib.

8. Place the ribs directly on the grill/smoker or griddle and sear for 10 to 15 minutes, until the ribs reach your desired crispiness, adding additional sauce as needed for burnt end results.

9. Let rest for 10 minutes, then serve hot.

PRO TIPS

To start peeling the membrane from the ribs, use a butter knife and wedge it right in the middle of the rack and once you've got it started, grip the membrane with a paper towel and remove it. The membrane will be too slippery to pull off the rack with just your fingers.

Place the individual ribs on a hot griddle or in a cast-iron skillet to sear off for 2 to 3 minutes to get burnt end results.

Griddled Burnt End Pineapple Chipotle Baby Back Ribs

SERVES 4

In 2022, we got a call from our friends at FOX to provide food for their summer concert series. This meant a 4 a.m. call time to prepare food for guests, crew, FOX hosts, band members, and anyone else who wanted assorted breakfast options (that really weren't always breakfast foods) for fifteen weeks during the summer. We got the call on Tuesday, May 17, and the first concert was Friday, May 26. Without seriously thinking it through, we quickly said, "YES, we'll do it!" . . . then hung up the phone and thought, *What have we just signed up for?*—but we haven't looked back since.

We literally had nine days to pull it off, but within a few days, we'd pulled together an all-star team—Masterbuilt Grills & Smokers, Lane's BBQ sauces & spices, Halteman Family Meats, and our friend and talented chef Sarah Zeller Possenti. This was the first recipe we prepared for our FOX summer concert journey, and it was the perfect thing to kick off what has become an awesome partnership between *FOX & Friends* and The McLemore Boys.

Apple wood chunks

2 slabs baby back ribs

Lane's BBQ Sweet Heat Rub/ Seasoning

½ cup liquid butter or 1 stick salted butter, melted

½ cup brown sugar

2 cups Lane's BBQ Pineapple Chipotle sauce

1. Set a grill/smoker to 225°F and add the wood chunks.

2. Prep the ribs by pulling the membrane off the back side. Season liberally with BBQ rub.

3. Place the ribs on the middle rack of the grill/smoker and cook for 2 hours.

4. Remove the ribs, add the butter, brown sugar, and half the BBQ sauce to the top side of the ribs, and then double wrap in aluminum foil.

5. Place them back on the middle rack of the grill/smoker and cook at 225°F for 1 hour more.

6. Remove the ribs and unwrap them. Raise the grill temp to 600°F or high heat.

7. Cut the slabs into individual ribs, place them in a pan, and toss with remaining sauce.

8. Grill the ribs over direct heat for 5 to 10 minutes, until they reach the desired crispiness.

9. Remove, let rest for 10 minutes, and serve hot.

PRO TIPS

To start peeling the membrane from the ribs, use a butter knife and wedge it right in the middle of the rack and once you've got it started, grip the membrane with a paper towel and remove it. The membrane will be too slippery to pull off the rack with just your fingers.

Rick's BBQ Slaw Dog

SERVES 8

Pulled pork is something we do more than any other recipe. It's easy, it's foolproof, and it goes a long way with the crowds we feed. We've served it up every way imaginable, so why not on a hot dog bun with coleslaw? We got our slaw recipe from our buddy Rick Reichmuth, a chief meteorologist at FOX. Rick is a great friend who we've done so much with over the years at FOX—this recipe came together like a cool breeze thanks to his help and friendship!

2 pounds Smoked Triple-Threat Pork Butt (page 173)

8 hot dog buns

8 ounces shredded cheddar cheese

2 cups coleslaw (see page 171)

Lane's BBQ Southbound Sauce

1 (32-ounce) jar hamburger pickles

1. Set a grill to 350°F.

2. Put 4 ounces of the pulled pork on each bun. Top the pork evenly with the cheese.

3. Put the buns on the grill for 3 to 5 minutes.

4. Pull off the grill and add the slaw, then finish with BBQ sauce and pickles to taste.

Rick's Slaw

1 head purple cabbage, shaved

2 carrots, shaved

1 large shallot or ½ onion, minced

1 cup Duke's mayonnaise

⅔ cup apple cider vinegar

2 tablespoons Dijon mustard

2 tablespoons honey or sugar

1 tablespoon liquid aminos

Kosher salt and black pepper

In a large bowl, stir together the cabbage, carrots, shallots, mayo, vinegar, mustard, honey, and liquid aminos. Season with salt and pepper to taste. Cover and refrigerate until ready to serve. The slaw keeps well in the fridge for a few days.

PRO TIPS

The extra juices left behind by the smoked pork can be used in sauces, soups, stews, and chili and can even add moisture to mashed potatoes or rice.

Smoked Triple-Threat Pork Butt

SERVES 12

We love pulled pork almost as much as we love our friend and FOX cohost Ainsley Earhardt. At the end of some of our Friday concerts we would send her home with an extra tray of this pulled pork and Lane's Southbound BBQ sauce to remind her of her South Carolina roots. We love that we share faith, family, and then the rest; so thanks, Ainsley.

Hickory wood chunks

¼ cup kosher salt

¼ cup coarsely ground black pepper

¼ cup smoked paprika

2 tablespoons garlic powder

1 (6- to 8-pound) bone-in pork shoulder

½ cup soy sauce

½ cup Worcestershire sauce

½ cup teriyaki sauce

Meat syringe

12 buns

Rick's Slaw (page 171), for serving

Your favorite BBQ sauce, for serving

1. Set a grill/smoker to 350°F and add the wood chunks.

2. In a small bowl, combine the salt, pepper, paprika, and garlic powder. Apply the seasoning mix to all sides of the pork butt.

3. Place the pork butt on the middle rack of the grill/smoker and place an aluminum pan below it to collect the drippings. Smoke for 30 to 35 minutes per pound, or until the internal temp reaches 160°F.

4. Pull the pork butt and the pan of drippings from the grill/smoker. Save 1 cup of the drippings and discard the rest.

5. Place the pork butt in a 9 x 13-inch aluminum pan. In a medium bowl, combine the soy sauce, Worcestershire, teriyaki, and the reserved drippings. Using a syringe, inject half the marinade throughout pork butt.

6. Place the pork butt (still in the pan) back on the middle rack of the grill/smoker and smoke for an additional 2 hours, or until the internal temperature reaches 202°F, basting every 30 minutes with the remaining marinade.

7. Remove from the grill/smoker, cover with aluminum foil, and let rest for 1 hour before shredding.

8. Pull and shred the pork, mixing in all drippings collected in the pan.

9. Serve with buns, Rick's Slaw, and your favorite BBQ sauce.

Burnt End Boston Butt Bites

SERVES 8

Everyone loves these savory, crispy burnt end bites, and through the years we've perfected them to serve when we gather and grill. At the Fox Nation Patriot Awards in Nashville hosted at the Grand Ole Opry, we served our fellow patriots and our Fox fans. We were so honored to give back to the patriots who have served and allow us all to live in the greatest country on earth. We also made this recipe at the FOX All-American Summer Concert Series on Father's Day for the VIPs and all the dads. There's nothing better than great BBQ and good music anywhere, anytime.

1 (4-pound) boneless Boston butt

¼ cup yellow mustard

¼ cup BBQ rub (your favorite kind)

5 to 6 tablespoons salted butter, cut into tablespoons

Honey

BBQ sauce

Brown sugar

1. Set a grill/smoker to 250°F.

2. Trim the fat off the pork butt and place the meat in a 9 x 13-inch aluminum pan. Coat the pork with the mustard and BBQ rub.

3. Smoke in the pan on the middle rack for 2 to 3 hours, or until the internal temperature reaches 160°F.

4. Cut the meat into 1½-inch cubes and place in a new aluminum pan. Pour some, but not all, of the juices from the first pan over the meat. Put the pats of butter on top. Drizzle with honey and BBQ sauce to taste. Sprinkle brown sugar on top.

5. Wrap the top of the pan in aluminum foil and smoke for 1½ hours more.

6. Pull the pan from the grill/smoker, remove the foil, and stir. Remove the excess juices and drizzle more BBQ sauce on top.

7. If you have a griddle, set it to high heat or 600°F and griddle the bites for 5 to 10 minutes, until your desired sizzle is reached. If you don't have a griddle, sear the bites in a large cast-iron skillet on the stovetop over medium-high heat.

8. Remove and enjoy!

PRO TIPS

You can modify this recipe to your liking—whether you like it saucy, sweet, tangy, or spicy, you can control the taste, so do it your way! Use a hot and spicy rub or BBQ sauce to kick it up a bit.

NASHVILLE, TN

FOX NEWS

MCLEMORE CHEFS JOIN F&F LIVE IN NASHVILLE

Honey-Glazed Bacon-Wrapped Hot Dogs

SERVES 4

This recipe takes hot dogs to a whole new level. We place them on a stick, wrap them in bacon, add smoke, and drizzle them with honey, and the result is magical. When they're finished off with creamy mustard, who needs a bun? It's a blend of sweet and tangy that is so very different from your traditional grilled or boiled hot dog.

8 hot dogs

8 (12-inch) wooden skewers

1 pound thick-cut bacon

1 cup honey

8 long hot dog buns (optional)

Creamy Mustard Sauce
   (page 84)

1. Set a grill/smoker to 300°F.

2. Pierce each hot dog through with a wooden skewer. Spiral cut the hot dog on the skewer.

3. Wrap the hot dog in bacon (one piece should be enough) and secure with toothpicks at each end.

4. Place the hot dogs on the grill/smoker and place a pan under them to catch the drippings. Smoke for 30 minutes, or until the bacon is golden brown, drizzling with honey every 10 minutes.

5. Turn the grill up to 450°F and cook until the bacon is crispy, drizzling with honey and flipping every 3 minutes until desired bacon crispiness.

6. Remove the toothpicks and serve on the skewers with mustard sauce for dipping, or put on hot dog buns for a traditional bite.

Smoked Pork Crown Roast

SERVES 12

If there was ever a meal fit for a king or queen, this is it. We first tested this recipe while camping in north Alabama for John II's and Whit's birthdays. We then took it and presented this to the FOX hosts at the We The Kingdom concert in 2022 and they loved it. The concert was amazing, one that we will remember for a lifetime. It's always nice when you meet people that share the same Christian values as you do and can share great food together as well. Life is so good, and we are blessed to be able to share it with all of you. If you're looking for a great recipe that will impress your guests because of how insanely awesome it looks, this crown roast is a go-to. And it tastes pretty good, too.

2 bone-in pork tenderloins

Lane's BBQ Spellbound Rub/ Seasoning

1 package stuffing mix

1. Set a grill/smoker to 275°F.

2. Place the pork fat-cap-side down on a cutting board and slice a few inches into the meat between each bone, being careful not to slice all the way through. Begin turning the pork into the crown (or a circle). If it's still not coming together, make the slices just a little bit deeper.

3. Season liberally with BBQ seasoning, making sure to get some inside each cut.

4. Begin to form into a crown and tie the crown together in a circle, using as much kitchen twine as needed. If not coming together, make the slices just a little deeper. Place the roast in a large cast-iron skillet. (This will help hold the roast together and will hold in the stuffing later.)

5. Smoke the crown roast on the middle rack for 2 to 3 hours, or until the internal temperature reaches 130°F.

6. Meanwhile, prepare the stuffing according to the package instructions.

7. Remove roast from heat and put your stuffing in the crown roast.

8. Place the roast back on the smoker and smoke for 45 minutes to 1 hour more, or until the internal temp reaches 145°F.

9. Remove from the grill and transfer to a cutting board, then cut the twine and slice the roast into chops between each bone. Serve with a scoop of stuffing on top.

PRO TIPS

Have your local butcher prepare the crown roast and tie it up for you!

PRO TIPS

Place the racetrack on a pizza stone or pizza pan on the grill to allow indirect heat to properly bake the dough to an even golden brown.

The easiest chicken to pull is a rotisserie chicken, so if you're short on time, grab one at the grocery store and pull it—no one will ever know!

If you're cooking this in a pizza oven, bake for 15 to 20 minutes.

Baked Racetrack Pulled Pork and Chicken

SERVES 8

The 2023 Daytona 500 was another great race and a good time spent with *FOX & Friends* and FOX Weather. All our camping neighbors came to hang out and enjoy some good food, share stories, and talk trash about our drivers. Camping in the infield is always fun, and this year was no exception. It was especially cool hanging with the Travis Pastrana team, the 12-and-under junior race teams, and all the camping buddies we meet each year. This recipe was one of the crowd favorites from the race because it's NASCAR-inspired, and it's a great recipe to do with the kiddos!

1 cup your favorite BBQ sauce, plus more for serving

Kosher salt and black pepper

1 pound your favorite pulled pork recipe

1 pound shredded chicken (see page 180)

2 (8-ounce) tubes refrigerated crescent rolls

1½ cups shredded Colby Jack cheese

1 cup pickled banana peppers

Liquid butter or 1 stick salted butter, melted

1. Set a grill/smoker to 400°F. Line a baking sheet with parchment paper.

2. In a large bowl, mix together the BBQ sauce and salt and pepper. Add the pork and chicken and coat with the sauce.

3. Unroll the crescent rolls, separating each triangle. Arrange them on the prepared baking sheet in a sunburst pattern, with the pointy ends of the triangles facing outward and the bases of the triangles overlapping in the center.

4. Layer some of the cheese evenly over the base of the triangles, then top with the pork and chicken, more cheese, and the banana peppers. Fold the triangle tips over the filling (there will be gaps where the ingredients peek out between triangles).

5. Spray the dough with butter and bake for 30 to 35 minutes, until golden.

6. Serve with more BBQ sauce.

Smoked Ham with Dr Pepper Glaze

We're all about tradition in the McLemore family, and that includes how we "pig" out on hams. Our moms and grandmas have been baking hams for generations with the same tried-and-true method—low and slow. Sure, it takes a while to bake, but the results are worth it! The sugar caramelizes on the ham, and we add a little bit of smoky goodness when we put it on the smoker. A new tradition for the McLemore family is getting to serve this amazing ham recipe in New York at the All American Christmas at Fox Square with our new Wonder Bread friends and family.

Apple wood chunks

1 (12-pound) precooked bone-in picnic ham

2 (12-ounce) cans Dr Pepper

2 cups brown sugar

1 cup honey

1 cup spicy brown mustard

½ cup maple syrup

1. Set a grill/smoker to 225°F and add the wood chunks.

2. Score the ham with 1-inch squares, ½ inch deep, and place in a 10 x 15-inch pan. (Scoring the ham not only gives it a festive look, it also allows the glaze to elevate the flavor of the meat.)

3. In a medium bowl, stir together the Dr Pepper, brown sugar, honey, mustard, and maple syrup. Pour the mixture over the ham. Save ¼ cup honey and mustard to mix together for honey mustard sauce.

4. Smoke in the pan on the middle rack for 3 to 4 hours.

5. Serve with honey mustard sauce.

PRO TIPS

IN THE KITCHEN: You can bake this in the oven if you're wanting to stay inside—just place the pan on the middle rack and bake at 225°F for 3 to 4 hours.

Family-Style Low Country Boil

SERVES 24

Sometimes we cook up a Low Country boil for a small crowd, but more often for a big one. At the McLemore house or at the hunting camp, when the word gets out that we're doing a boil, the crowd usually grows. For us, the more the merrier, and we have a method for how to handle it. If you have the right equipment with an extra-large pot, you're covered. Back in our Masterbuilt days, we would use our Masterbuilt Indoor Electric Fryer, which also allowed us to steam and boil. If you don't, simply use this method to cook the ingredients separately and you'll get it done. Separating the ingredients also allows those with food allergies to enjoy this yummy recipe!

10 ounces shrimp-and-crab-boil seasoning (boil bags)

6 pounds red potatoes

3 pounds yellow onions, halved

6 lemons, halved

Liquid butter

Kosher salt and black pepper

24 frozen short ears corn

6 pounds precooked sausage, cut into 2-inch lengths

10 pounds easy-peel large shrimp

Cajun seasoning

Cocktail sauce, for dipping

3 large (19.5 x 11.5-inch) aluminum pans (sizes may vary)

1. Set a Masterbuilt Electric Fryer, Boiler, and Steamer to high and fill with 3 gallons water. (Be sure to follow your boiler's capacity instructions.)

2. Add half the shrimp and crab boil seasoning to the water and bring to a boil. Add the potatoes, onions, and lemons and boil for 30 minutes, until the potatoes are fork-tender.

3. Drain the potatoes, onions, and lemons from the basket, pour them into a large aluminum pan, and coat with butter, salt, and pepper to taste. Cover with aluminum foil to steam and keep warm.

4. Add corn and boil for 30 minutes. Drain the corn from the basket, pour into pan, and coat with butter, salt, and pepper to taste. Cover with aluminum foil to steam and keep warm.

5. Add the remaining boil seasoning to the water, then add the sausage and boil for 6 minutes. Add the shrimp and continue boiling for 4 minutes.

6. Turn the unit off and let the sausage and shrimp sit in the water for an additional 3 to 5 minutes.

7. Drain, pour into the pan with the potatoes, and season with Cajun seasoning to taste. Cover for 10 minutes.

8. Uncover and serve with cocktail sauce for dipping.

PRO TIPS

This recipe is so good there may not be any leftovers, but if there is be sure and check out our Low Country Boil Goulash on page 217.

Steamed Snow Crab Legs

SERVES 8

The best way to enjoy crab legs is to find a $9.99 all-you-can-eat buffet and eat so many that they ask you to leave. Just kiddin'. The best way is to steam them yourself at the same time you do a Low Country Boil (see page 184) for a complete seafood feast. We have steamed crab legs and boiled seafood all over the country from the Florida beach all the way up to Pennsylvania at QVC promoting the Masterbuilt Electric Fryer, Boiler, and Steamer. This recipe is sure to keep you from feeling crabby when you shell out some good vibes as you gather and grill.

3 ounces Old Bay seasoning

6 lemons, cut in half

8 to 10 pounds snow crab legs

1 stick salted butter

1. Set a Masterbuilt Electric Fryer, Boiler, and Steamer to high with 1 gallon water. Add the seasoning and lemons to the water and bring to a boil.

2. Place the crab legs in the basket and hook the basket in the steam position.

3. Close the lid and steam for 20 minutes.

4. Put the butter in a small saucepan and bring to a low boil, then remove from the heat. Strain into a bowl for dipping.

PRO TIPS

Adding 1½ teaspoons of cornstarch to every ½ cup of butter will help separate the butter for easier and faster clarifying.

Johnboy's Smoked Lemon Salmon with Bourbon Glaze

SERVES 4

John II has been working over the years to perfect a smoked salmon recipe. While on a production set working with the Masterbuilt marketing team, he was food styling for a new grill that was being launched and tried a version of this recipe because the color looks so good on camera. Well, according to the team that was on set, this ended up being the best salmon they had ever tasted, so it became a winner. John II will always be called Johnboy by his mom, so we named this recipe after him. They both love salmon, and they love cooking it together. Cooking as much as we do, eating healthy is very important—and doing it with your mom is important, too.

1 large salmon fillet

Kosher salt and black pepper

Garlic powder

1 cup brown sugar

1 stick salted butter

2 lemons

Bourbon glaze (optional)

1 tablespoon minced fresh parsley, for garnish

1. Set a grill/smoker to 225°F.

2. Lightly coat a baking sheet with olive oil and place the salmon fillet skin-side down on top of a small layer of aluminum foil. Lightly coat the rest of the salmon fillet with olive oil.

3. Season lightly with salt, pepper, and garlic powder to taste.

4. Sprinkle the brown sugar evenly over the fillet.

5. Cut the stick of butter into ¼-inch-thick pats and arrange them evenly on top of the fillet.

6. Cut 1 lemon in half and squeeze the juice evenly over the entire fillet. Cut 2 or 3 thin slices from the second lemon and place them on top of the fillet; cut the remaining lemon into wedges and reserve for serving.

7. Place the salmon fillet on the middle rack and smoke for 30 minutes.

8. Raise the temperature on your smoker to 350°F and cook for 15 to 20 minutes more. If you like, add a light layer of your favorite bourbon glaze to the top of the fillet during this final 15 to 20 minutes. Once the albumin—aka the white stuff—has started oozing out, remove the salmon from the grill/smoker. If not, check every 5 minutes until you see it and then remove.

9. Let the smoked salmon rest for 5 minutes. For additional flavor, pour the juices from the baking sheet over the fillet. Garnish with the parsley. Serve with lemon wedges on top!

PRO TIPS

IN THE KITCHEN: You can easily do this in a skillet on your stovetop (we always recommend a cast-iron skillet). Be sure to give the skillet time to fully heat up before searing the tuna.

Seared Ahi Tuna

SERVES 4

Ariel Abergel is a FOX producer and a great friend of the McLemores. We love going to FOX when he is producing our segments. Ari takes really good care of us while we're there, so when we got a request from him to cook some tuna, we jumped at the chance. The result is this delicious recipe especially because it is "so hard" to do—just kiddin'. Thanks, Ari, for all the help over the years, and more importantly, thanks for the friendship.

2 (8-ounce) sashimi-grade ahi tuna fillets

Extra-virgin olive oil

Kosher salt and black pepper

Garlic powder

Sesame seeds (optional)

Soy sauce, for serving

Teriyaki sauce, for serving

Wasabi (optional)

1. Heat a griddle to high and get it as hot as possible.
2. Lightly coat the tuna with olive oil. Season with salt and then with pepper, followed by garlic powder to taste.
3. Sear the tuna for 20 to 25 seconds on each side.
4. Remove, add a light layer of sesame seeds, if you like, and cut the tuna into thin slices across the grain.
5. Enjoy with soy sauce and teriyaki for dipping. A little wasabi also pairs great with this tuna!

Pawpaw's Campfire Baked Grouper

SERVES 4

We will never forget all the things that Ole Man/Pawpaw taught us growing up, and we can always look back on those fond memories with a smile on our faces. He truly is an amazing man, who taught us how to work hard, always do what you say, and never tell a lie unless it's about the size of the fish you caught. If it wasn't a successful fishing trip, you can always just cook the vegetables in this recipe without the fish. When we would get back to camp and make this meal, we would sit around a "campfire" and tell stories that are forever burned into our memories. Thanks, Ole Man/Pawpaw, for giving us an amazing life and for making us into the men we are today.

4 (½-pound) grouper fillets

1 pound golden potatoes, finely diced

1 large yellow onion, finely chopped

2 sticks butter, 16 pats

4 garlic cloves, finely chopped

Kosher salt and black pepper

1. Set a grill/smoker to 350°F or prep your campfire if you want to go traditional.

2. Place two pieces of aluminum foil in a cross and put 1 fillet in the center. Cover the fillet with one-quarter of the potatoes and onion. Place 4 pats of butter on top. Cover with one-quarter of the garlic cloves. Season with salt and pepper to taste. Fold all four ends of the foil into the center, creating a boat to hold in the juices. Repeat to make three additional boats.

3. Place the foil-wrapped fillets above coals of your fire or on direct heat of your grill and cook for about 30 to 40 minutes, depending on how hot your coals are may change the time.

4. Turn over to allow the juices to mix, then put back on the coals or grill for 15 minutes more.

5. Remove from the grill/smoker or campfire and serve from the foil wraps.

PRO TIPS

This works even better on the Masterbuilt Gravity Series Grill because you can control the cooking temperature. We recommend cooking it over direct heat at 350°F for 30 to 45 minutes.

Griddled Shrimp and Grits

SERVES 8

Because we're from the South, we're used to seeing grits on every menu, so having shrimp and grits in this cookbook was a must. We've cooked shrimp every way you can think of, so why not with grits and a few onions and peppers? And true to our roots, we had to throw in some bacon, because it wouldn't be the same at the McLemore house if it didn't have bacon.

1 pound bacon, cut into 1-inch pieces

1 stick butter

2 cups grits

1 green bell pepper, chopped

1 yellow bell pepper, chopped

1 red bell pepper, chopped

1 small yellow onion, chopped

2 cups heavy cream

4 cups chicken broth

2 cups 2% or whole milk

2 pounds large raw shrimp, peeled (tails removed) and deveined

Kosher salt and black pepper

Cajun seasoning

Garlic powder

1. Heat a griddle to high. Griddle the bacon to a relatively crispy doneness, then drain on paper towels, chop into large bits, and set aside. Save the bacon grease.

2. In a medium saucepan add ¼ stick of butter and sauté the bell peppers and onion over medium heat. Add ½ cup of the cream, reduce the heat to low, and simmer to thicken.

3. In large pot, combine the broth, remaining 1½ cups cream, the milk, and the remaining ¾ stick of butter and bring to a boil over high heat. Add the grits and cook for 5 minutes, stirring every minute, then cover. Reduce the heat to low and let sit while you cook the shrimp. Add salt and pepper to taste.

4. Season the shrimp with Cajun seasoning and garlic powder to taste and griddle on high for 5 to 6 minutes. You'll know your shrimp are cooked perfectly when they change color to white and pink and curl up, but the trick is to watch the thickest part of the shrimp. When that part turns from translucent to opaque white, it's done.

5. Pour the grits into bowl and top with the shrimp, bacon, and peppers.

PRO TIPS

Feel free to "Southern up" this recipe a bit more by adding your favorite cheese to the grits.

Tonya's Lemon Pepper Tilapia

SERVES 4

Tonya has cooked tilapia for us for as long as we can remember. What we all remember most was watching her season it directly on the countertop, then pan-fry it on the stove, making a huge mess in the process. A mess that was worth it because we absolutely loved it. Now we help Mom out by baking the tilapia on the grill and adding that extra bit of flavor that only a grill can add.

8 thin boneless tilapia fillets

Liquid butter

Lemon pepper seasoning
(we recommend Lane's BBQ
Sweet Lemon Pepper Rub/
Seasoning)

4 lemons, cut in half

1. Set a grill/smoker to 350°F.

2. Line a baking sheet with aluminum foil and place the tilapia on the foil. Lightly coat with butter and season with lemon pepper seasoning.

3. Roast on the grill/smoker on the middle rack for 30 to 35 minutes, until flaky and cooked through.

4. Pour all juices from tilapia, butter, and seasoning into a small bowl for a dipping sauce.

5. Remove and squeeze lemon juice over the top.

PRO TIPS

IN THE KITCHEN: Feel free to cook the tilapia in the oven at 350°F for 30 to 35 minutes if you don't want to go to the grill.

Lining reusable pans with foil helps with cleanup without compromising cooking. We often line the bottom of our smokers with foil, too.

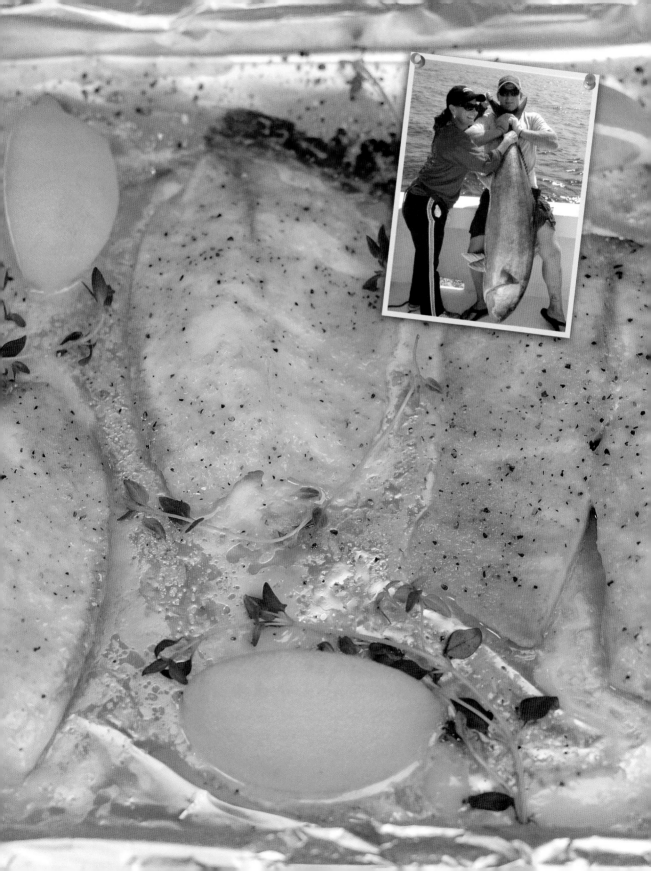

PRO TIPS

IN THE KITCHEN: Feel free to sear your scallops in a cast-iron skillet on the stovetop if you don't have a griddle at the house.

Sea scallops have a side muscle that needs to be removed before cooking. If your fishmonger has not done it already, pinch the flap between your thumb and finger and pull it away—it's that easy!

Griddled Seared Scallops

SERVES 4

John II and Tonya love scallops and will order them at restaurants any chance they get. When we decided to add this recipe to the cookbook, Tonya insisted on taste testing it to make sure it was done right. John II has been working to perfect searing scallops, and we think we have a winner here. Apparently, we did it right, because we got her approval!

1 stick salted butter

Kosher salt and black pepper

Garlic powder

2 lemons

1 pound fresh sea scallops

Extra-virgin olive oil

White wine (optional)

1. Melt the butter in a small saucepan or in a bowl in the microwave. Add the salt, pepper, garlic powder, and the juice of 1 lemon and stir to combine for butter mixture.

2. Put the scallops in a bowl and pour over the butter mixture, coat, and mix thoroughly. Cover and refrigerate for 1 hour.

3. Heat a griddle to high and oil it well.

4. When the griddle is hot, add the scallops and sear for 2 to 3 minutes, flipping every minute and basting with the butter mix, until tender and dark brown on top. If desired, add a light splash of white wine while searing to help tenderize the scallops.

5. Remove and serve with quartered lemons for squeezing.

Reverse-Seared Lamb with Mediterranean Sauce

SERVES 4

When country music artist Michael Ray performed at one of the 2022 FOX summer concerts, lamb was on the menu. Our friend and Master Chef Tony Seta hooked us up with enough lamb to feed everybody there, from the VIPs to the FOX hosts to the entire band. The Mediterranean sauce mixed with a perfectly reverse-seared lamb chop roast was almost as big a hit as Michael's music!

For the Mediterranean Sauce

1½ cups sunflower oil

⅓ cup fresh lemon juice

¼ cup white balsamic vinegar

3 tablespoons minced garlic

3 tablespoons minced red onion

2 tablespoons dried oregano

1 tablespoon brown sugar

2 teaspoons sea salt

2 teaspoons black pepper

1 teaspoon red pepper flakes

1 teaspoon fennel seeds, crushed

For the Lamb

1 (8-bone) rack of lamb

½ cup Lane's BBQ Brancho Combo Rub

1. Make the Mediterranean sauce: In a large bowl, stir together all the ingredients for the sauce until well combined. Set aside.

2. Make the lamb: Set a grill/smoker to 275°F.

3. Season the lamb liberally with Brancho rub. Smoke for 1½ hours, or until the internal temp reaches 130°F, basting with the sauce every 20 to 30 minutes.

4. Remove and let rest for 10 minutes. Turn the grill up to 600°F.

5. Cut the lamb into 8 individual chops and baste the cut sides with the sauce.

6. Sear for 1 minute per side, or until the chops reach the desired internal temp (see Pro Tips).

7. Remove from the grill and baste again with the Mediterranean sauce before serving.

PRO TIPS

We know that lamb is not technically wild game, but it sounds like it should be.

Internal Temperatures:

- Medium-rare: 145°F
- Medium: 160°F
- Well-done: 170°F

Stuffed Venison

The McLemores all grew up hunting for most of our childhoods. Spending time at deer camp was fun and kept us out of trouble for sure. As we all got older, we tried to continue the tradition and hunt together as a family. Our schedules make that hard sometimes, but we go as much as we can because we enjoy the thrill of the hunt. If we're not writing cookbooks, traveling around the world, or working on a tractor, we try to hunt. Our buddy Glenn Garner supplied us with this recipe that we used to cook a buck Bailey had taken, and it turned out amazing. Thanks, Glenn!

Apple wood chunks

4 (½-pound) venison tenderloins

BBQ rub

1 (8-ounce) block cream cheese, softened

4 mild jalapeños, seeded and finely chopped

1 pound thin-sliced bacon

1. Set a grill/smoker to 350°F and add the wood chunks.

2. Cut each tenderloin into 8-inch lengths and butterfly lengthwise. Season with BBQ rub.

3. Stuff each tenderloin with ¼ cup of the cream cheese. Top the cream cheese with the jalapeños.

4. Close the venison around the filling and wrap each tenderloin with 3 strips of bacon. Secure with 5 toothpicks and season with BBQ rub again.

5. Place directly on the grill/smoker and cook for 35 to 40 minutes, flipping every 10 minutes, until the internal temperature reaches 130°F.

6. Remove and cut between each toothpick to serve.

Grilled Brined Quail

SERVES 4

Quail hunting is a great sport that we do from horses or 4-wheel-drive open rigs, or while walking. The key to a good hunt is the dogs that do all the work and the handlers that work the dogs. There is a very serious safety aspect that everyone knows. Whatever you do throughout the hunt, DO NOT shoot . . . the dog. You can shoot your friend, even the guide, but you had better not shoot the dog if you want to get invited back. So, after a good hunt and no one getting shot, we clean the birds and throw 'em on the grill. You know you've had a great day hunting when it ends on the back deck eating what you just cleaned and telling stories with your buddies about who had the best shot.

3 lemons, halved

1 cup kosher salt, plus more
  as needed

½ cup brown sugar

¼ cup honey

3 tablespoons black pepper,
  plus more as needed

2 carrots, sliced

2 celery stalks, sliced

1 onion, diced

Bay leaves

½ cup fresh parsley

½ ounce fresh thyme

1 head garlic, cut in half

8 quail, spatchcocked
  (see page 142 or 145) or
  de-breasted (see Pro Tip)

Your favorite sweet BBQ sauce

1. Fill a 4-quart saucepan with 8 cups water and add all the ingredients except the quail and BBQ sauce. Bring to a boil over high heat, then reduce the heat to maintain a simmer and cook for 3 minutes. Remove from the heat and let the brine cool for 1 hour.

2. Pour the brine into a container large enough to hold the liquid and the quail. Add enough ice water to the brine to cover the quail, cover, and refrigerate overnight.

3. Set a grill to 350°F.

4. Remove the quail from the brine and season lightly with salt and pepper to taste.

5. Grill for 5 to 7 minutes on each side, until the internal temperature reaches 160°F.

6. Remove and sear whole breast filet with your favorite sweet BBQ sauce.

PRO TIPS

Quail is a smaller bird, so it's easier to overcook. Brining provides protection against the undesirable effects of overcooking and adds extra flavor to the meat. To de-breast bird, simply cut from the top of the breast bone down both sides to remove breast fillet.

Grilled Wild Turkey Fingers

SERVES 8

Turkey hunting is an addictive sport—once you get hooked, it's hard to not let it control your time during the short season. We have a lot of friends in the hunting business here in Hamilton, Georgia, so we never have to worry about running short of wild turkey. The question is, how do we cook it? If we deep-fry a turkey, it is typically a domestic bird. If it's a wild turkey, we will smoke it or, in this case, throw it on the grill. Either way, it's good, but the time spent hunting and cooking with friends is the best part.

1½ cups Sprite
(one 12-ounce can)

1 cup soy sauce

½ cup balsamic vinegar

½ cup olive oil

1 tablespoon prepared horseradish

1 tablespoon minced garlic

2 teaspoons kosher salt

1 (4-pound) wild turkey breast, cut into strips

1 bushel pack 8 romaine hearts

Alabama White Sauce
(page 80), for drizzling

1. In a 1-gallon zip-lock bag, combine the Sprite, soy sauce, vinegar, olive oil, horseradish, garlic, and salt. Add the turkey, seal the bag, and place in a pan in case it leaks. Refrigerate for at least 4 hours or up to overnight.

2. Set a grill/smoker to 400°F.

3. Remove the meat from bag and discard marinade then grill the turkey for 8 to 10 minutes, or until the internal temp reaches 160°F.

4. Serve the turkey on lettuce, drizzled with white sauce.

PRO TIPS

Store-bought turkeys are preinjected with brine and are therefore more forgiving. Brining wild game is a crucial step that you do not want to overlook for more juicy and flavorful results!

Bacon-Wrapped Dove Kabobs

SERVES 8

Ned Yost is known in baseball for being with the Atlanta Braves and a World Series Champion as a manager with the Kansas City Royals. But he's known to us as a friend who loves to hunt, work on his farm, and cook up some good food. Ned has hunted doves on our farm, and we have hunted on his, and the stories run wild from each hunt, from which farm had the most birds to who had the best shot of the day. What's so interesting about hunting with your friends is not who's the best shot, but who's the best storyteller. We would put *all* our money on Ned!

Hickory wood chunks

16 dove breasts
(32 breast nuggets)

1 pound thin-cut bacon,
halved lengthwise

8 long wooden skewers

DADGUM Good Seasoning
(page 87), or your favorite
brown sugar–based rub

1. Set a grill/smoker to 350°F and add the wood chunks.

2. Wrap each dove piece with bacon and slide onto a skewer, 4 pieces per skewer. Season liberally.

3. Grill for 15 to 18 minutes, then flip and grill for 15 to 18 minutes more, until the bacon begins to crisp up and the internal temp reaches 165°F.

4. Remove and serve off the skewer!

Roasted Smoked Wild Duck

SERVES 8

Duck is something you typically go to a high-end restaurant to eat. Unless you're a die-hard duck hunter or have the chance to find a place to hunt, it's not something you cook daily. We hunt deer, turkey, dove, quail, squirrel, and occasionally rabbit, but duck hasn't been on our list quite as much because we didn't have a duck pond. We decided to change that and build our own spot to hunt ducks. Part of the fun is building the pond, the other part is the hunt, but the best part is smoking the ducks after a successful day in the blind with a few good ole friends.

1 (5-pound) wild duck

2 cups Korean bulgogi
   BBQ sauce

1 orange, cut into wedges

1 lemon, cut into wedges

1 lime, cut into wedges

Apple wood chunks

2 cups orange juice

1. Using a fork, poke holes through the skin of the duck over the entire bird.

2. Place the duck in a 1-gallon zip-lock bag and add 1½ cups of the BBQ sauce and the orange, lemon, and lime wedges. Seal the bag and place in a pan in case it leaks. Refrigerate overnight.

3. Set a grill/smoker to 350°F or medium heat and add the wood chunks.

4. Place the duck on the middle rack and place a pan underneath. Pour the orange juice into the pan. Cook for 4 hours, or until the internal temperature reaches 145°F, brushing with the remaining BBQ sauce every 15 minutes.

5. Remove the pan from underneath the duck and grill for an additional 30 minutes to crisp up the skin.

6. Pull duck and let rest until the internal temperature reaches 160°F.

7. Carve and serve.

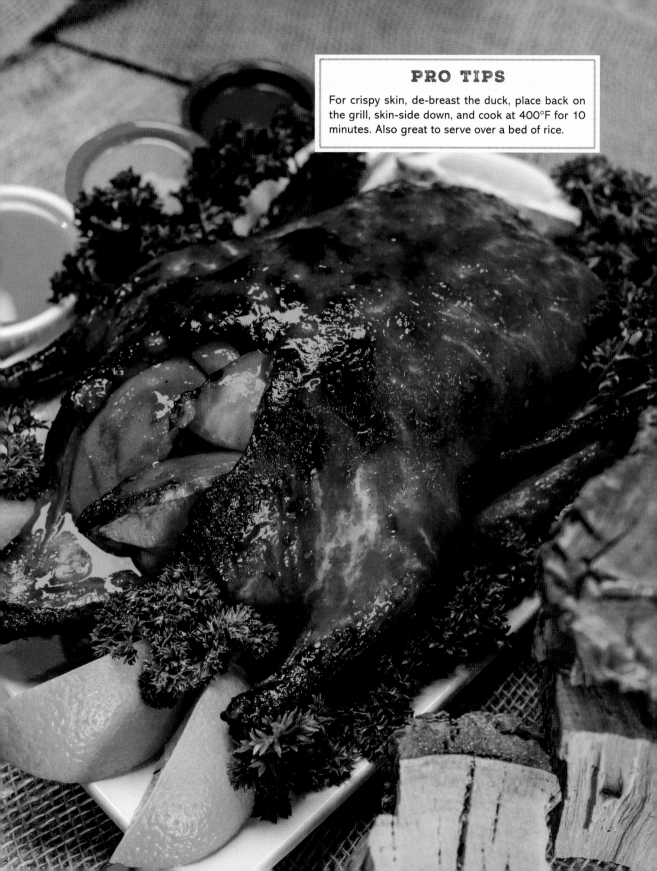

PRO TIPS

For crispy skin, de-breast the duck, place back on the grill, skin-side down, and cook at 400°F for 10 minutes. Also great to serve over a bed of rice.

Smoked Bunny and Dumplings

SERVES 8

We have cooked just about anything, anywhere. So when our buddy Steve Harvey called in the experts—The McLemore Boys—to help him do an episode of his talk show called "Taste Like Chicken," we were up for the task. The challenge was to cook four things that Steve would blindly taste, and he had to guess what it was. We cooked frog legs, snake, gator tail, and rabbit. The rabbit was prepared with dumplings, and it was our favorite—it seemed to be Steve's as well. We have enjoyed a good friendship with Steve over the years from cooking at his Boys Mentoring camp at his farm in Texas, doing his radio and TV shows, and sharing recipes together. Thanks, Steve, for being one of the funniest guys we know and for all you've done for so many people. Cooking rabbit is like cooking chicken, so don't be intimidated—give it a try!

1 (5-pound) whole rabbit

Olive oil, just a dab

Kosher salt and black pepper

Garlic powder

Paprika

8 cups (64 ounces) chicken broth

1½ cups (12 ounces) frozen premade dumplings

3 cups (32 ounces) frozen mixed vegetables (we prefer a mix of corn, peas, carrots, green beans, and lima beans)

1. Set a grill/smoker to 275°F.

2. Coat the rabbit with a layer of olive oil. In a small bowl, mix salt, pepper, garlic powder, and paprika and season the rabbit completely.

3. Smoke for 1 hour, or until the internal temperature reaches 160°F. When done, discard the skin and remove all the meat from the bones, placing the meat in a separate bowl. Discard the bones and shred the meat.

4. While the rabbit is smoking, place a large cast-iron pot on stove, add the broth, and bring to a boil over high heat.

5. Add the dumplings to the broth one at a time and gently stir to keep them separate. Boil for 15 minutes, then add the vegetables and reduce the heat to maintain a simmer.

6. Add the rabbit to the dumplings and simmer for 20 to 30 minutes more to thicken.

PART 6
LEFTOVERS

At the McLemore house, we are the kings and queens of leftovers. We intentionally cook extra for this very purpose. It's never an indication that the original meal wasn't good. We do not throw anything away—not only does it save us money, but it gives us the opportunity to get creative and try to put another spin on an already good recipe. Leftovers are a way to enjoy a recipe we love in a new way—on a sandwich, in a salad, or in a goulash. Besides just putting leftovers in the microwave again, these recipes will have you looking forward to having yesterday's meal again, but with a twist.

Low Country Boil Goulash

Because we so often cook for large crowds—and we have a big family—leftovers are a big thing at the McLemores'. Tonya always wants to make the most out of every meal, and we love the challenge of finding ways to use leftovers from our demos at FOX, parties at the house, and testing recipes for our cookbooks. Instead of letting the food go to waste or just heating it up, we get creative and add to the already good recipes to make them even better. After all, the best meals are the ones you create sometimes by accident. Our Low Country boil is a perfect example of a recipe we always have extra of, and this goulash is a great way to keep enjoying it long after the party is over.

Family-Style Low Country Boil
leftovers (page 184)

4 tablespoons (½ stick) salted
butter

Kosher salt and black pepper

1 cup sour cream

1 cup shredded sharp cheddar
cheese

1. Slice the potatoes into ¼-inch-thick slices. Chop the onions into 1-inch pieces. Cut corn kernels off the cobs. Cut the sausage into ½-inch pieces. Peel the shrimp and cut them in half.

2. In a large cast-iron skillet, sauté on the stove or on your grill all the ingredients together with the butter and salt and pepper to taste for about 10 minutes.

3. Add the sour cream, stir, and then top with cheese. Place on the grill or back in the oven at 350°F for 15 minutes.

Smoked Chicken Salad Lettuce Wrap

YIELD VARIES DEPENDING ON YOUR LEFTOVERS.

We always love seeing Janice Deen as we check out the weather at FOX in NYC. She brings a smile and personality that makes the day sunny, even when it rains. She loves our food and tries her best to eat healthy so this recipe helps do just that. Smoked chicken is always on rotation at our house, and it never disappoints our family and Janice approves as well. We plan ahead and cook extra to have leftovers to make sandwiches, put in our Brunswick stew, and make this delicious chicken salad. This is so good, we find ourselves forecasting smoked chicken just to make this dish.

Grilled Spatchcocked Chicken (page 145)

1 cup mayonnaise

1 cup pecans, chopped

1 cup finely chopped celery

1 (5-ounce) bag dried craisins

4 tablespoons (½ stick) butter, melted

1 teaspoon kosher salt

1 teaspoon black pepper

½ teaspoon Cajun seasoning

2 packs romaine hearts (6 to 8 heads)

1. Finely chop the leftover chicken to yield 3 to 4 cups. Place the chicken in a large bowl and add the mayo, pecans, celery, craisins, melted butter, salt, pepper, and Cajun seasoning.

2. Cut the lettuce into pieces the size of your hand.

3. Place 2 tablespoons of the chicken salad in a piece of lettuce and roll into a wrap. Enjoy!

Smoked Brisket Sandwich with Come Back Sauce

"Holy moly, this is the best sandwich we have ever had." This is the response we got at the Talladega 500 while cooking for the *FOX & Friends* team. The Comeback Sauce is so DADGUM good that it makes you come back for more!

Our friend Tim Van Doran, aka Bama Grill Master, stopped by to share some stories and hang out. We also got to spend some time together in the Florida Keys at the "Rub and Tug Invitational" raising awareness for Pediatric Cancer Research. Tim competed and won while we did a segment on *FOX & Friends* to help educate the public about this worthy cause. One thing is for sure, when it comes to gathering and grilling Bama Grill Master is one of our go-to guys!

3-Step Brisket (page 111),
    16 leftover slices needed

Kosher salt and black pepper

16 slices provolone cheese

8 large slider buns, split,
    or 16 slices brioche

Come Back Sauce (page 83)

Favorite BBQ sauce

1 head iceberg lettuce,
    shredded

1 large tomato

1. Set a grill/smoker to 350°F.

2. Thinly slice the brisket or just grab whatever leftover slices you
    have already cut.

3. Fold each slice in half and place on a baking sheet. Season with
    salt and pepper to taste and then place 2 slices of the cheese on
    top of each slice.

4. Place on the grill/smoker on the middle rack and cook until the
    cheese has melted.

5. Toast the rolls on the grill and spread both sides with Come
    Back Sauce.

6. Build each sandwich on the rolls with the cheesy brisket, BBQ
    sauce, lettuce, tomato, and more salt and pepper to taste. Serve
    and enjoy.

Mac and Cheese Brisket Sandwich

YIELD VARIES DEPENDING ON YOUR LEFTOVERS.

Mac and cheese and brisket are two of the most popular recipes we make when we gather and grill, so pairing them together just seemed to be a good idea. Turns out we were right, so pairing this Texas recipe with our Texas friend and *FOX & Friends* cohost Will Cain seemed like the perfect fit. Will loves football and eating which makes him an honorary McLemore Boy. PS: Roll Tide! Just kiddin', Will. Go Longhorns! We had to put this recipe in the cookbook.

1 baguette

Smoked Jalapeño Mac and Cheese (page 53), or regular mac and cheese

3-Step Brisket (page 111), sliced

Kosher salt and black pepper

1. Set a grill/smoker to 350°F.

2. Cut the baguette into 5-inch-long pieces, then cut in half to make sandwich bread.

3. Warm up your mac and cheese and brisket slices by placing them on the grill/smoker over indirect heat for 10 to 15 minutes. Brisket can go directly on the middle rack; place the mac and cheese in a cast-iron or heat-resistant bowl.

4. Toast the baguette slices while warming up the other ingredients, then build your sandwiches with the brisket and mac and cheese and enjoy!

PRO TIPS

Feel free to simply microwave the mac and cheese and brisket slices for convenience; we've done it and we won't tell anyone!

Ham and Potato Combo

From time to time, we get asked, "How do you come up with your recipes?" Throughout our travels, we learn from all the people we meet, family and friends, and sometimes we simply throw things together and hope they work. This recipe was one that we actually experimented with while writing this cookbook. We had leftover ham and potatoes along with other ingredients lying around the kitchen. We smashed it all together and put it on the grill for hours while testing other recipes, and WOW, it turned out to be a winner.

3 tablespoons olive oil

1 large onion, chopped

2 cups diced celery

2 cups diced carrots

2 pounds leftover Smoked Ham (page 182), cut into ¾-inch cubes

2 pounds red potatoes, cut into ¾-inch cubes

1 large (27-ounce) can turnips (optional)

4 cups (32 ounces) pork broth or chicken broth

Bread, for serving

1. Set a grill/smoker to 350°F.

2. In a large cast-iron pot on the stovetop, heat the olive oil over medium heat. Add the onion, celery, and carrots and sauté for about 5 minutes or until they soften.

3. Add the ham, potatoes, turnips (if using), and broth and bring to a boil. Stir and cook for 15 minutes more.

4. Place the pot on the grill/smoker over indirect heat and cook, uncovered, for 3 hours, stirring occasionally.

5. Remove from the grill, stir, and smash the potatoes.

6. Serve with your favorite bread.

PRO TIPS

IN THE KITCHEN: This can be done in the oven or in a slow cooker! Simply add all ingredients together and slow cook in the oven for 1 hour at 350°F or in your Crock-Pot for 4 to 6 hours on High.

Smoked Pork Fried Rice

SERVES 8

We love going out to eat at all the local Asian restaurants when we travel. This leftovers recipe is one that reminds us of those local spots, and now allows us to enjoy the cuisine at home. We also love how it helps us pull any and everything out of the refrigerator to stir-fry together. If you don't have pork or chicken, it tastes just as good with steak, brisket, or even sausage.

The secret to great fried rice is using cold leftover rice. Left in the fridge overnight, the rice grains will firm up, making them easier to separate and decreasing the chances of the rice turning out mushy. Fried rice is the ultimate leftovers dish.

Extra-virgin olive oil

1 cup diced carrots

1 cup sweet peas

½ cup diced white or
   yellow onion

4 tablespoons (½ stick) butter

Store-bought instant white rice

2 pounds Smoked Triple-Threat
   Pork Butt, shredded
   (page 173)

4 large eggs, beaten

¼ cup soy sauce

¼ cup oyster sauce

Kosher salt and black pepper

Chopped fresh chives,
   for topping

Alabama White Sauce (page 80)

1. Heat a griddle to high. Coat the griddle with olive oil and sauté the carrots, peas, and onion until soft, 6 to 8 minutes, then push them to the side of the griddle.

2. Melt the butter on the griddle, add the rice, then add the pork and mix together.

3. Mix all the ingredients together on the griddle and create a hole in the center for the eggs.

4. Scramble the eggs and stir-fry all together until all the ingredients are thoroughly cooked through, 6 to 10 minutes.

5. Add the soy sauce and oyster sauce to taste, season with salt and pepper, and completely blend together.

6. Serve in small bowls, topped with chives and white sauce to taste.

PRO TIPS

Feel free to heat your leftover pulled pork in a cast-iron skillet on the stovetop (or secretly just heat it all up in the microwave).

Make your own quick-pickled red onion by thinly slicing a red onion. In a small saucepan, combine 1 cup of red wine vinegar, ¼ cup of sugar, and 1 tablespoon salt and boil until the sugar dissolves, about 2 minutes. Add the onion and boil for another 2 minutes, then remove from the heat and let cool in the liquid. Drain, and serve the pickled red onion on the tacos.

Sarah's Pulled Pork Tacos

SERVES 6

The most talented chef and food stylist we know is our friend Sarah Possenti. It's not just her ability to cook amazing food that makes us look good, but her ability to create and style food like no one else we know. Her food is always fun, creative, unique, and DADGUM good. This recipe is a perfect example of her genius. We owe a lot of credit to Sarah for helping us prepare food when we share it with all of you. When we travel to New York to cook for *FOX & Friends* or cook on location at the Super Bowl or a NASCAR race, she is always there to help. Thanks Sarah, we love you and your family for always helping The Mc-Lemore Boys look good!

2 pounds Smoked Triple-Threat Pork Butt (page 173)

½ cup your favorite BBQ sauce (we love Lane's BBQ Pineapple Chipotle sauce)

1 cup Mexican mix shredded cheese or crumbled Cotija cheese

12 soft flour taco shells

2 cups coleslaw, store-bought or homemade

½ cup pickled red onion

Chopped fresh cilantro (optional)

1. Heat a griddle to medium. Toss the pulled pork with the BBQ sauce until completely coated, mixed and heated up.

2. Put some of the cheese in a taco shell, top with the pulled pork, coleslaw, pickled red onion, and cilantro, if desired, and enjoy!

Ole Man's Leftover Salmon and Eggs

Dawson McLemore, aka Ole Man, has been the most influential man in our lives. As children growing up, we all remember our camping, fishing, and hunting trips from the back of our truck camper and little fishing boat. We wouldn't trade the memories for anything. What we also remember, like it was just yesterday, was working together with him and calling him Daddy or Dad at work and it being slightly weird. We never wanted to be disrespectful and call him by his first name, so we gave him the nickname "Ole Man" (not *old* man), and it stuck. One day while talking to him about his campfire grouper recipe (page 192), he also turned us on to the perfect leftover salmon recipe. We loved it so much that it made the cut for this cookbook and room for another story to remember with the Ole Man.

2 cups (12 to 16 ounces) shredded leftover smoked salmon (see page 187)

4 large eggs, beaten

Kosher salt and black pepper

¼ cup shredded cheddar cheese

Chopped fresh chives, for serving (optional)

1. Set a grill/smoker or even your oven to 400°F.

2. Layer the shredded salmon over the bottom of an 8-inch cast-iron skillet. Pour the eggs over the salmon and season with salt and pepper.

3. Bake for 20 minutes, or until the eggs are done to your liking.

4. Add the cheese and bake for 3 to 5 minutes more to melt the cheese.

5. Remove from the grill and top with chives, if you like.

PRO TIPS

You can use store-bought canned salmon in this recipe if you don't have leftover salmon handy!

Most cast-iron skillets come preseasoned, meaning they're ready for cooking as soon as you take them out of the box. However, over time the seasoning erodes and you need to reapply it by brushing the skillet with a thin layer of neutral oil and heating it until the oil bonds to the metal. In this recipe, the salmon is oily enough to keep it from sticking.

PART 7

DESSERTS

We all know that DESSERTS spelled backward is STRESSED. But the way to not be stressed is to eat more desserts! We hope that our desserts here do just that for you—make you feel better. Most BBQ experts don't think that desserts can be done on the grill, but in the McLemore family, we enjoy pushing the boundaries and trying new things! You'll never know if you don't try!

PRO TIPS

Add fruit, chocolate, whipped cream, or Nutella to make this dessert even more decadent. Also, we recommend using disposable aluminum trays for easy cleanup or to send leftovers home with a friend, if there's any left.

Bailey's French Toast

SERVES 8

Bailey is the youngest of the McLemore third generation and is probably the most *well rounded* of us all. Born on Valentine's Day in 1998, she completed the family. She is a teacher like her mom and her sister, Brooke; she is an incredible singer and leads worship at our church; she plays all kinds of sports; and she's probably the best all-around cook in the McLemore family. She has the natural ability to cook things that make us wonder why she doesn't have her own bakery. This dessert ranks as one of the best we have ever had. It's so good, we had her make it in New York at one of the FOX summer concerts. She served it to the hosts, the VIPs, the FOX crew, and the band members. After they tasted it, they asked Bailey if she would go on the road with them. Her brother said yes, and her dad said no. Sorry, we don't mind sharing her desserts, just not her.

For the French Toast

6 medium eggs, beaten

1 cup milk

½ cup heavy cream

½ cup granulated sugar

1 tablespoon ground cinnamon

1 tablespoon vanilla extract

1 loaf Italian bread, sliced 1 inch thick

For the Crumble

1 cup all-purpose flour

½ cup brown sugar

½ teaspoon salt

1 stick butter, cubed and softened

1. Make the French toast: Set a grill/smoker to 350°F. Grease a 3-inch-deep 9 x 13-inch pan with PAM.

2. In a large bowl, whisk together the eggs, milk, cream, granulated sugar, cinnamon, and vanilla.

3. Soak the bread in the egg mixture and place it in the prepared pan, lining the pan with the slices at an angle. Pour the remaining egg mixture over the bread in the pan.

4. Make the crumble: In a small bowl, combine all the crumble ingredients. Spread the crumble evenly over the French toast.

5. Bake on the grill/smoker on the middle rack for 40 to 45 minutes, until golden brown.

Bailey's Cinnamon Roll Monkey Bread

SERVES 8

Bailey followed in her mom's and sister's footsteps by becoming an elementary school teacher. Like we mentioned in her French toast recipe on page 235, she is a DADGUM good cook. If she's not singing us a song at the house or at church, she's teaching us how to make great desserts! Whenever there's a family gathering, we always beg her to whip up one of her desserts with her special caramel sauce. We call it liquid gold because it tastes just that good. When she puts it on top of this monkey bread or drizzles some over ice cream or uses it as a dip for fresh fruit, we can't get enough! We all know that Bailey is the best baker around, and when she brings out her desserts with liquid gold, there's always an "OooOOooo" in the room. If you want something sweet and delicious—just like Bailey—make this bread with some of her legendary caramel sauce. You won't regret it!

1 stick unsalted butter, melted, plus 1 tablespoon softened butter for the pan

3 (8-ounce) cans cinnamon rolls with icing

½ cup granulated sugar

1½ teaspoons ground cinnamon

⅓ cup brown sugar

1 teaspoon vanilla extract

1. Preheat the oven to 350°F. Coat the inside of a 10-inch Bundt pan with the tablespoon of softened butter.

2. Open the cinnamon rolls and set the icing aside. Cut each roll into 6 pieces and make sure none are sticking together.

3. In a medium bowl, mix the granulated sugar and cinnamon together and roll the cinnamon roll pieces in the cinnamon-sugar to coat.

4. In a microwave-safe bowl, melt the butter, then add the brown sugar and vanilla.

5. Drizzle one-third of the brown sugar mix over the bottom of the pan.

6. Layer half the cinnamon roll pieces in the pan, then drizzle with another third of the brown sugar mix. Layer the remaining cinnamon roll pieces and press them into the pan so the top is even. Drizzle the remaining brown sugar mix over the top.

7. Bake for 45 to 50 minutes until golden brown. Remove from the oven and let cool for 15 minutes, then flip the bread out onto a plate and drizzle the icing over the top.

Bailey's Caramel Sauce

½ cup granulated sugar

½ cup brown sugar

1 stick unsalted butter

¼ cup heavy cream

1. In a nonstick medium pan, combine all the ingredients and heat over medium-high heat, whisking continuously, until the mixture comes to a boil, about 3 minutes. Make sure to whisk continuously to prevent the caramel sauce from burning. This is a sauce you cannot walk away from.

2. Remove from the heat and pour into a bowl, then serve.

PRO TIPS

Put the softened icing in a zip-lock bag and cut off the tip of one corner for easy drizzling (that's a redneck piping bag right there!). Feel free to bake this on the middle rack of your grill/smoker if you want that additional smoky flavor.

Smor'dilla

SERVES 12

This is a recipe that the McLemore family has been doing for years! When we were researching dessert ideas for this cookbook, we found an old YouTube video that John did with the girls. Masterbuilt and the marketing team were launching a new grill about fifteen years ago and we chose to grill this recipe in the backyard. Fast-forward to when we were camping and tailgating in New York at FOX News, yes, in FOX Square, and wanted s'mores, because you can't camp without s'mores, right? We couldn't have a fire in Midtown New York, so we made s'mores on the grill to make us feel like we were camping in the woods. You don't have to be at a campfire to enjoy s'mores with the kids. This is a great dessert that's quick and super easy to make and can be enjoyed anywhere.

12 soft tortilla shells—the bigger, the better!

6 milk chocolate bars, broken into 6 small squares per taco

6 cups small marshmallows (½ cup per taco)

Chocolate syrup, for topping

1. Set a grill or griddle to medium heat.

2. For each smor'dilla, place a tortilla on the grill, add your chocolate squares and marshmallows, and fold the tortilla in half. Flip and grill until both sides are golden brown and the fillings have melted.

3. Drizzle with chocolate syrup and serve.

PRO TIPS

Adding some crumbled graham crackers to the filling really creates that s'mores experience!

Feel free to experiment with the quantities of chocolate and marshmallows for your desired level of sweetness.

You can also experiment with adding other types of chocolate or crushed-up candy bars inside the tortilla.

PRO TIPS

Feel free to use store-bought brownie mix, but the point here is that cooking them on a grill in a cast-iron skillet gives your brownies that extra smoky flavor!

Instead of using the traditional egg mixture, substitute ½ cup sweetened condensed milk for a gooier brownie!

Grilled Skillet Brownies

Keeping with tradition, brownies are good when they are served—anytime, any-place. Grilled Skillet Brownies served hot with ice cream are even better. For some reason, things just taste better when they're cooked outside on a grill. It probably has something to do with the friends and family who've gathered with you and helped you make them. Anything served with the folks you love is always better.

Hickory wood chunks

1 cup sugar

1 stick butter, melted

2 large eggs

⅔ cup unsweetened cocoa powder

½ cup all-purpose flour

¼ teaspoon baking powder

½ teaspoon salt

1 cup walnuts, chopped

½ cup chocolate chips

Chocolate syrup, for topping

Ice cream, for serving

1. Set a grill/smoker to 350°F and add the wood chunks.

2. In a 10-inch cast-iron skillet, thoroughly mix together the sugar, butter, and eggs. Add the cocoa powder, flour, baking powder, salt, and walnuts and mix to combine. Top with the chocolate chips.

3. Baked on the middle rack of the grill/smoker for 30 to 40 minutes. Don't overbake! Use a toothpick to check the doneness of your brownies at 30 minutes and every few minutes after. If you stick the toothpick in and it comes out clean, the brownies are done!

4. Drizzle with chocolate syrup and serve with ice cream.

Grilled Blueberry Cobbler

SERVES 8

In our first cookbook, *DADGUM That's Good*, we have an amazing blackberry cobbler recipe. We modified it here to use blueberries, bake it on the grill, and of course top it with vanilla ice cream. Making dessert on the grill is perfect. We prep the dessert before we sit down to eat, start the baking while we eat, and when we're done eating, the dessert is hot and ready for everyone to enjoy. Sometimes we even dress up as blueberries just for fun!

1¼ cups sugar

1 cup self-rising flour

1 cup half-and-half or heavy cream

1 stick butter, melted

3 cups fresh blueberries

Vanilla ice cream, for serving

1. Set a grill/smoker to 350°F.

2. In a medium bowl, mix 1 cup of the sugar and the flour together and blend in the cream and melted butter.

3. Place the blueberries in 10-inch cast-iron pan or 9 x 13-inch aluminum pan. Pour the flour mixture over the berries and sprinkle the remaining ¼ cup sugar on top.

4. Place on the middle rack and grill, with the lid closed, for 45 minutes to 1 hour, until golden brown on top. Start checking the cobbler at 45 minutes.

5. Remove from the grill and let set for 10 minutes, then serve hot, with ice cream.

> ## PRO TIPS
>
> **IN THE KITCHEN:** You can always cook this cobbler in the oven the traditional way, just follow the same times and temps, but don't forget that doing it on the grill gives it that extra bump of smoky flavor.

Grilled Apple Pie

Apple pie is America's dessert, so we knew we didn't want to leave it out of our first McLemore Boys cookbook. As the best baker in the family, we knew Bailey was the right person to call for tips for this recipe. Thanks to her, it turned out perfectly! Like most traditionally baked recipes cooking them in the oven is great but spice it up and add that backyard flavor by trying it on the grill. You'll *apple*-solutely love it!

Apple wood chunks

6 Granny Smith or other green apples, peeled, cored, and cut into wedges

½ cup lemon juice

1 tablespoon cornstarch

3 tablespoons cold water

4 tablespoons (½ stick) butter

¾ cup light brown sugar

¼ cup granulated sugar

1 teaspoon ground cinnamon

1 teaspoon vanilla extract

1 tablespoon Lane's BBQ apple pie seasoning

About ¼ cup amaretto liqueur

2 store-bought piecrusts

Vanilla ice cream, for serving

1. Set a grill/smoker to 350°F and add the wood chunks.

2. Place the apples in a large bowl and coat with the lemon juice; set aside.

3. In a small bowl, mix the cornstarch and 3 tablespoons cold water to create a slurry; set aside.

4. In a 12-inch cast-iron skillet, melt the butter over medium heat. Add the brown sugar, granulated sugar, cinnamon, vanilla, and apple pie seasoning, then stir in the slurry to thicken the mixture.

5. Add the apples and cook, stirring, for 10 minutes to soften the apples, then add a splash of the amaretto and cook for an additional 5 minutes.

6. Line a pie pan with one of the piecrusts and pour in the apple mixture before they cool completely.

7. Layer the second piecrust on top and crimp the edges with a folk. Cut a few slits in the top for venting steam.

8. Place on a warming rack and grill for 40 to 45 minutes, until the crust is golden brown.

9. Remove, let rest for 10 minutes, and serve with vanilla ice cream.

Banana Nut Loaf

At the McLemores', we are often guilty of not eating the bananas that Tonya buys. It's not because we don't like fresh bananas or that we don't want to eat healthy, we just simply forget. Tonya, being the leftover-food police, will not let us throw anything away, so we make this banana nut bread with our very ripe bananas. Baking it on the grill is a-*peeling*, always serves up well, and doesn't hurt Tonya's *peelings*.

Nonstick cooking spray (optional)

4 ripe bananas

1½ cups self-rising flour

3 medium eggs, beaten

1 stick salted butter, melted, plus butter for serving

1 cup granulated sugar

½ cup brown sugar

½ cup pecans, chopped

1 cup walnuts, chopped

½ cup chocolate chips

½ cup vegetable oil

1 tablespoon vanilla extract

1 teaspoon ground cinnamon

1 teaspoon baking soda

1. Set a grill/smoker to 350°F. Line a 9 x 5-inch loaf pan with parchment paper or spray with cooking oil to prevent sticking.

2. In a large bowl, mash the bananas. Add the flour, eggs, melted butter, granulated sugar, brown sugar, pecans, walnuts, chocolate chips, vegetable oil, vanilla, cinnamon, and baking soda. Thoroughly mix and blend the ingredients together.

3. Pour the batter into the prepared pan and bake for 35 to 40 minutes, until a skewer inserted into the center comes out clean.

4. Cut into 1-inch-thick slices and serve warm with butter and your favorite cup of coffee.

Lynne's Georgia Peach Cobbler

SERVES 8

As John and his brother Don grew their families, family time always centered around the family business, Masterbuilt. Don's wife, Lynne McLemore, was the CFO for over ten years and is one of the smartest people we know. She helped us build an amazing company, and was always the one who kept us straight with finances and did it with a smile. Don and Lynne got married in May 1988 and John and Tonya in August 1988. They worked together and raised their kiddos together while loving every minute of it. Before Brooke and Bailey started "adulting" and helping with food at family functions, Lynne was the OG dessert queen. She has perfected many sweet treats that have graced our dinner table for the past thirty-five years. She and Don are so fun to be around, and we never take for granted how lucky we all are to have been in business together for so long and still want to hang out every chance we get. So, thanks, Lynne, for this peach of a recipe, but more importantly, thanks for the memories.

6 fresh peaches, peeled, pitted, and diced

1¼ cups sugar

1¼ sticks salted butter

1¼ cups milk

1¼ cups self-rising flour

Vanilla ice cream, for serving

1. Set a grill/smoker to 350°F.
2. Place the peaches in a 1-gallon zip-lock bag, add half the sugar, seal the bag, and toss to coat. Refrigerate overnight.
3. Remove the peaches from the fridge and let them come up to room temperature before baking.
4. In a 12-inch cast-iron pan, melt the butter over medium heat. Add the milk, sugar, and flour and blend together. Add the peaches and top with remaining sugar.
5. Grill for 45 minutes to 1 hour, until browned.
6. Remove and let cool. Serve with vanilla ice cream.

PRO TIPS

Cobblers can be made with many fruits. Try berries like blackberries or raspberries, or stone fruits like plums, or even apples or pears. Heck, mix all your fruits together—you know where we're going with this . . . have fun!

PRO TIPS

Add hickory chunks for extra flavor.
These are also good deep fried; not as healthy, but DADGUM good.

DADGUM Good Donut Bites

SERVES 8

Our first three cookbooks, *DADGUM That's Good*, *DADGUM That's Good, Too*, and *DADGUM That's Good . . . and Healthy!*, were fun to write and even more fun to promote. We traveled the country in and out of every TV station, radio station, and magazine company that would have us, promoting cookbooks and our family business, Masterbuilt. We served fried donuts as a way to promote not only our cookbooks, but our deep fryers. Now we're offering another way to cook these a-*glazing* donuts—baking them on the grill! *Donut* worry or be *glazed* and confused—these are sure to be your jam!

1 (8-ounce) can biscuits (not flaky)

¼ cup sugar and 1 tablespoon cinnamon, mixed

1 (8-ounce) can sweetened condensed milk

¼ cup powdered sugar

1. Set a grill/smoker to 400°F.

2. Cut each biscuit into quarters. Lightly coat with the cinnamon-sugar.

3. Place the biscuits on a baking sheet sheet and bake for 16 to 18 minutes, until golden brown.

4. Remove from the grill and drizzle with the condensed milk. Dust with the powdered sugar and serve.

FOX CONCERT SERIES RECIPES BREAKDOWN

2022

» Week 1: Griddled Burnt End Pineapple Chipotle Baby Back Ribs

» Week 2: Canceled due to the Queens Jubilee

» Week 3: 3-Step Brisket: Trim, Season and Smoke

» Week 4: Smoke 'n' Seared Burnt End Wings

» Week 5: Burnt End Pork Belly Bites

» Week 6: Seared Skirt Steak Tacos with Corn Salsa and Chimichurri

» Week 7: Double Bacon and Cheddar Smash Burger

» Week 8: Reverse-Seared Tomahawk Steak

» Week 9: Bacon Pig Shots

» Week 10: Smoked Pork Crown Roast

» Week 11: Reverse-Seared Lamb with Mediterranean Sauce, with Chef Tony

» Week 12: Smoked Loaded Glizzy

» Week 13: Seared Ahi Tuna Medallion

» Week 14: Griddled Donut BLD

» Week 15: Austin, Texas, with Lee Brice

2023

» Week 1: Griddled Smashed Mini Cheeseburger Sliders (Memorial Day)

» Week 2: Smoked BBQ Meatloaf Minis

» Week 3: Smoked BBQ Brunswick Stew

» Week 4: Bone-In Rotisserie Pork Roast (Father's Day 2023)

» Week 5: Bacon-Wrapped Cheeseburger Pizza Fatty

» Week 6: Smoked Honey-Glazed Spareribs (Fourth of July)

» Week 7: Smoked Brisket Sandwich with Come Back Sauce

» Week 8: Baked Pork Breakfast Fatty (July 14)

- » Week 9: Baked Personal Pizza Rolls (July 21)

- » Week 10: Smoked Jalapeño Bacon Mac and Cheese

- » Week 11: Baked Breakfast Croissant Ring

- » Week 12: Rotisserie Lemon Pepper–Brined Chicken

- » Week 13: Breakfast Quesadilla

- » Week 14: Smoked Triple-Threat Pork Butt

- » Week 15: Patriotic Red, White, and Blue Wings

2024

- » Week 1: *Fox & Friends* Traditional Smoked Ribs (May 24th, Memorial Day)

- » Week 2: Breakfast Fatty

- » Week 3: Smoked BBQ Nacho Bar

- » Week 4: Ultimate Smoked Breakfast Burger (Father's Day)

- » Week 5: Good Ole Boy Chicken Thighs (Sam's Recipe & Story)

- » Week 6: Smoked French Cut Prime Rib

- » Week 7: Sweet-and-Spicy Wings (Fourth of July)

- » Week 8: Smoked Whole Beef Tenderloin

- » Week 9: Double Trouble Brisket/Butt Hoagie

- » Week 10: Smoked Beef Ribs

- » Week 11: Griddled Chicken Fajitas

- » Week 12: Reverse-Seared Pork Tenderloin Sliders with Pickles and Come Back Sauce

- » Week 13: 60-Minute Grilled Ribs

- » Week 14: Rick's BBQ Slaw Dog

- » Week 15: Smoked Ham with Dr Pepper Glaze (Labor Day)

ACKNOWLEDGMENTS

We want to thank our family and friends who have helped us along the way to make our journey not only successful, but fun and memorable, too. For all the support every time we would get together to gather and grill. For every time we fire up the grill and smoker, set up the tables and tents, test a new recipe and turn on the cameras, The McLemore Boys say THANK YOU . . .

Thanks, Brooke, for bringing Brian into our lives, and for your two wonderful boys, Whit and Walt, with their cute smiles, and not to mention your famous Buffalo dip.

Thanks, Bailey, for finally figuring out how to be funny as the youngest and always bringing the absolute best desserts in the world for everyone to enjoy.

Thanks, Michael, for being the biggest SURPRISE in the family and bringing Jana and your three amazing kids, Abigail, Alanah, and Ben, into our lives.

Thanks, Ole Man, for starting it all and for bringing Cynthia into our lives. Most of all, thanks for teaching us the true meaning of what it means to be a man and how to follow our dreams.

Thanks, the second-generation McLemore siblings who were the original Masterbuilt workforce that helped make and shape our family legacy.

Thanks, Shirley, for bringing Tonya into our lives and for being a great mother-in-law and Mimi to all the grandkids.

Thanks, Sarah Zeller Possenti, for your friendship and teaching us your tricks of the trade and culinary skills.

Thanks, Chris Patchin and Media Mule, for being a great family friend and capturing our memories and stories.

Thanks, *FOX & Friends*, for helping us share our recipes and stories through the years. Whether in New York in FOX Square for a holiday, cooking for the VIPs at the summer concert series, on location at a Super Bowl game, or at a NASCAR race, thank you all for "Gathering at our Grill" with America.

Thanks, the HarperCollins family . . . Maddie Pillari, our editor, for your focus and expertise in editing this project and keeping us on track to meet the deadlines; Lisa Sharkey, for your creativity and trusting us to tell our story and share our secrets to the world. And the rest of the HarperCollins team: Lexie Von Zedlitz, Kyle O'Brien, Leah Carlson-Stanisic, Frieda Duggan, Tom Hopke, Theresa Dooley, and Joanne O'Neill, for allowing us to take this journey and share with all of you that want to Gather at your Grill with The McLemore Boys.

INDEX

(Page references in *italics* refer to illustrations.)

ABOUT THE AUTHORS

The McLemore Boys are a father and son duo who believe in Faith first, family second and then all the rest will fall naturally into place. John Sr, former owner, and CEO/President of Masterbuilt, spent his life running the family business with the Ole Man and his siblings. From the age of 15, John II began working his way from the warehouse to departments like customer service, product development and marketing for the company with his dream of working with his dad just like John Sr did with the Ole Man. Their love of food came from cooking in their backyard with the Ole Man and in the kitchen with MeMaw, family and friends, camping trips and testing the latest invention for the family business. Today, they travel the country as masters of everything grilling and smoking sharing some of their favorite recipes, most memorable stories, and life lessons with all of you. From national TV, radio, podcasts, and social media; to NASCAR races, Super Bowl's or charitable events, they love meeting new friends, learning new recipes and sharing their expertise with you.

HarperCollins books may be purchased for educational, business, or sales promotional use. For information, please email the Special Markets Department at SPsales@harpercollins.com.

FIRST EDITION

Designed by Kyle O'Brien

Art credits include Orange Pins: Lyudmyla Kharlamova/Shutterstock

Front and rear matter art:
romeovip_md/Shutterstock; All photos decor/Shutterstock;
Unchalee Khun/Shutterstock; Eliana Davis/Shutterstock;
Titus Group/Shutterstock; solarus/Shutterstock

Part One opener art: everydayplus/Shutterstock
Part Two opener art: Reinhold Leitner/Shutterstock
Part Three opener art: ilolab/Shutterstock
Part Four opener art: Andrey Skutin/Shutterstock
Part Five opener art: Ksw Photographer/Shutterstock
Part Six opener art: Krasovski Dmitri/Shutterstock
Part Seven opener art: balwanrai/Shutterstock
(Part Seven also found in Front Matter)

Library of Congress Cataloging-in-Publication Data has been applied for.

ISBN 978-0-06-335105-9

24 25 26 27 28 TC 10 9 8 7 6 5 4 3 2 1